Bistro

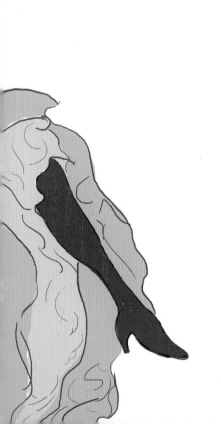

Bistro
Great French food

David Bransgrove

NEW HOLLAND

To my parents for showing me the value
of hard work
&
Whan for love and support

Contents

Bienvenue
Welcome

A bistro is like an old friend—as soon as you walk in, there is an air of familiarity, a sense that it's always been there and always will. Traditionally, a bistro is a small family-run establishment, serving timeless comforting classics and seasonal specialities in modest surroundings, all at a reasonable price. The service is fast and the prices are low. Bistros are run on a shoestring and turning tables is imperative. To be profitable, food needs to be simple and fast.

The bistro is a uniquely Parisienne invention and the origins of the word 'bistro' itself are surrounded by mystery and folklore. The most popular theory is that during the Russian occupation of Paris in 1815, hungry Cossacks would bang on the restaurant tables shouting 'Bystra' or 'hurry up' demanding quick service. This is unlikely to be true, since the first recorded bistro opened 70 years after they left. Another plausible origin is the abbreviation of the word *bistrouille*, a colloquial term for coffee mixed with poor-quality brandy, a drink likely to be served in a bistro.

Some say a traditional bistro is trapped in another era, a bit of a cliché, and that the terminology should apply randomly to any establishment where cheap, quick food is served. There are also places trading as bistros, capitalising on the nostalgic value, but falling well short on being reasonably priced. This is a great pity and I have fears that the term will eventually lose all meaning.

Paris, fortunately, is still a stronghold of the traditional bistro ethos.

The recipes in this book are just some of the many in the repertoire of every good bistro chef. This is food without pretense, no complicated techniques or expensive ingredients, just good honest home cooking.

That's what bistro food is.

Fonds et sauces
Stocks & sauces

Fumet de poisson
Fish stock

Makes about 1.25 litres (40fl oz)

500G (1LB 2OZ) FISH BONES
1 ONION, SLICED
1 LEEK, WASHED AND SLICED
1 FENNEL BULB, SLICED
1 BOUQUET GARNI

Buy a whole fish—use the fillets for another dish and the bones for the fumet.
Chop the fish bones into even 10-cm (2-in) pieces. Wash thoroughly. Combine all the ingredients in a saucepan and just cover with cold water. Bring to a gentle simmer and cook uncovered for 30 minutes. Pass the liquid through a fine sieve. Cool and refrigerate. The fumet keeps for 2–3 days.

Fond de volaille
Chicken stock

Makes 2 litres (70fl oz)

1KG (2LB 4OZ) RAW CHICKEN
   CARCASSES
1 ONION, PEELED AND HALVED
1 LEEK, TRIMMED AND HALVED
6 CLOVES GARLIC
2 CELERY STICKS, TRIMMED AND
   HALVED
1 BAY LEAF
6 WHITE PEPPERCORNS

Place the bones in a stockpot, cover them with cold water and bring to the boil. Skim off any fat and impurities. Add the vegetables peeled and split in half. Bring back to the boil and simmer, uncovered, for 5 hours. Pass the liquid through a fine sieve. Cool, then refrigerate. It will keep for 3 days in the fridge.

Fond de boeuf
Beef stock

Makes 2 litres (64fl oz)

To make a quality stock you need quality bones. Use bone, such as shin cross cuts or oxtail that have a good quantity of meat. The roasted flesh will give colour and flavour, while the slowly cooked connective tissues will add body.

1KG (2LB 4OZ) BEEF BONES

1 ONION, CHOPPED

1 CARROT, CHOPPED

250ML (8FL OZ/1 CUP) RED WINE

6 CLOVES GARLIC, WHOLE

½ BUNCH THYME

1 BAY LEAF

6 BLACK PEPPERCORNS

Preheat the oven to 200°C (400°F). Place the bones on an oven tray and roast for 1 hour until evenly browned.

In a large stockpot heat 200 ml (7fl oz) of the fat from the roasting tray. Add the onion and carrot and fry on a high heat until deeply caramelised. Pour in the wine and reduce to a syrup.

Add the bones to the pot with the remaining ingredients. Fill the pot with enough cold water to cover the bones and bring to the boil. Reduce to a simmer. Cook uncovered for 10–12 hours, skimming off any fat and scum as necessary. Keep topped up with water as required.

Pass the liquid through a fine sieve into a clean saucepan and reduce by half, skimming off any impurities. Pass through a fine sieve again. Cool the stock, then refrigerate. It will keep for 3 days in the fridge.

Mayonnaise

Makes 250ml (8fl oz/1 cup)

An indispensable sauce, mayonnaise is used as is or as a base for many derivatives. In essence, it is just an emulsion of oil and egg yolk. Mustard adds flavour and also aids the emulsion. This sauce is so simple to make and tastes nothing like the store-bought variety. Adding the oil in a thin drizzle and insuring all the ingredients are at room temperature reduces the likelihood of splitting.

2 EGG YOLKS

1 TEASPOON DIJON MUSTARD

185ML (6FL OZ/¾ CUP) VEGETABLE OIL

60ML (2FL OZ/¼ CUP) OLIVE OIL

1 TEASPOON WHITE WINE VINEGAR OR LEMON JUICE

SALT AND WHITE PEPPER

Whisk together the yolks and mustard. Start by adding the oil a few drops at a time; as you see it emulsifying you can add the oil in a more steady stream, whisking vigorously all the time. Add the vinegar and mix well. The sauce will be quite thick—add hot water to thin down if necessary. Season to taste.

If the sauce splits, it can be brought back by whisking together 1 egg yolk and ¼ teaspoon of mustard in a clean bowl and adding in the split sauce little by little. Remember the most common cause of splitting is cold ingredients.

Aïoli

Makes 550ml (19fl oz)

This classic Provençal sauce is so highly revered that it is also the name of a complete dish, in which the sauce is served with salt cod, eggs, snails and a whole array of vegetables. The method for making aïoli is the same as for mayonnaise.

6–8 CLOVES GARLIC, PEELED
½ TEASPOON SALT
2 EGG YOLKS
250ML (8FL OZ/1 CUP) VEGETABLE OIL
60ML (2FL OZ/¼ CUP) OLIVE OIL
1 TABLESPOON LEMON JUICE

Smash the garlic under the broad side of a large knife blade. Chop very finely and then crush with the salt to form a paste. Add this to a bowl with the egg yolks. With a whisk, work in the oils drop by drop until an emulsion begins to form, and then in a thin stream, whisking all the time. Add the lemon juice. Thin with a little hot water if the aioli is too thick. Check seasoning.

Alternatively, the sauce can be made using a food processor, starting with pureeing the garlic, salt and yolks, and then proceeding as normal.

Rouille

Essentially, rouille is a highly spiced, garlicky, saffron mayonnaise. Sometimes tomato is added or roasted peppers, or even a boiled sieved potato. This is a simplified version. It is the classic accompaniment to fish soup, but try it also with fish dishes and even lamb.

Follow the aïoli recipe, adding a large pinch of saffron threads steeped in 1 tablespoon of lemon juice to the garlic and egg yolks. Finish the sauce with ½ teaspoon of cayenne pepper.

Sauce remoulade
Mustard and pickles mayonnaise

Makes 1–1½ cups

Ths is a wonderfully piquant sauce which can be used to dress vegetables for salads, such as potatoes and celeriac, or with cold and fried fish. It's also a perfect accompaniment to some cold sliced meats, such as pickled veal tongue or corned silverside.

6 TABLESPOONS CORNICHONS, FINELY CHOPPED
2 TABLESPOONS CAPERS, FINELY CHOPPED
1 TABLESPOON DIJON MUSTARD
1 TABLESPOON PARSLEY, CHOPPED
250ML (8FL OZ/1 CUP) MAYONNAISE (SEE RECIPE, PAGE 12)

Make sure the cornichons and capers are well drained before chopping. Add them to the mayonnaise with the rest of the ingredients and mix well.

Vinaigrette

Makes 450ml (15fl oz/2 cups)

Vinaigrette is essential for dressing salad leaves or as a sauce for vegetable crudites.

160ML (5½FL OZ/⅔ CUP) VEGETABLE OIL
160ML (5½FL OZ/⅔ CUP) OLIVE OIL
2 TABLESPOONS WHOLEGRAIN MUSTARD
125ML (4FL OZ/½ CUP) WHITE WINE VINEGAR
SALT AND PEPPER

Combine all ingredients in a glass or plastic bottle. Simply shake together before each use. This is not an emulsified sauce and the ingredients will separate. Keep in the refrigerator.

VARIATIONS

Vinaigrette aux noix
Walnut vinaigrette

Substitute walnut oil for the olive oil. Use this for richer salads such as roquefort or beetroot.

Vinaigrette aux agrumes
Citrus vinaigrette

Replace the vinegar with equal an quantity of lemon, orange and grapefruit juice. Use it to dress grilled fish or salad leaves to accompany a duck confit.

Tapenade

Serves 6

This olive paste can be served as an hors-d'oeuvre with vegetables or on toasts with soup, particularly tomato. For a vegetarian version, omit the anchovies.

500G (17½OZ) BLACK OLIVES, PITTED
2 CLOVES GARLIC
2 ANCHOVY FILLETS
4 TABLESPOONS CAPERS
½ RED PEPPER ROASTED AND SKINNED
1 TABLESPOON THYME, CHOPPED
6 TABLESPOONS OLIVE OIL
1 TABLESPOON LEMON JUICE
PEPPER

Chop the olives, garlic, anchovies, capers and red pepper very finely (this is best done in a food processor). Add the thyme, olive oil and lemon juice. Season with pepper if desired.

Sauce hollandaise

Serves 4

This sauce has a fearsome reputation for being notoriously temperamental. If you follow these two simple rules it should be no problem. The egg yolks must be cooked until thick ribbon stage—that is, when you drag the whisk through the sauce, it is thick enough that a trail is left. And the cooked egg mixture and butter need to be the same temperature—about blood temperature.

It's great with poached or grilled fish and, of course, asparagus.

3 TABLESPOONS WHITE WINE

1 TABLESPOON WHITE WINE VINEGAR

1 SHALLOT (ESCHALOT), PEELED

4 PEPPERCORNS

200G (7OZ) BUTTER

3 EGG YOLKS

JUICE OF ½ LEMON

SALT

Combine the wine, vinegar, shallot and peppercorns in a saucepan. Bring to a simmer and reduce by half. Strain the liquid through a sieve and leave to cool.

Melt the butter in a saucepan, then remove from the heat and leave to settle. The melted butter will separate into two layers. Pour off the top yellow layer; reserve and keep warm. Discard the bottom milky substance.

Combine the wine reduction and the egg yolks in a heatproof bowl, then place the bowl over a saucepan of barely simmering water. Whisk vigorously until the mixture reaches the thick ribbon stage (see above). Remove from the heat and continue whisking until slightly cooled. Add the melted butter, very little at a time, whisking constantly until it is all incorporated. Whisk in the lemon juice and season with salt.

Serve immediately.

Sauce béarnaise

This derivative of hollandaise is classically served with grilled steak or chicken.

Simply add the stalks from ½ bunch of tarragon when making the wine reduction. Proceed as with hollandaise and finish the sauce with freshly chopped tarragon leaves.

Sauce maltaise

The arrival of the short-seasoned blood orange announces that spring is on its way. Use the sauce with asparagus or fish.

Instead of lemon juice, add the juice and grated zest of 1 small blood orange to a hollandaise sauce.

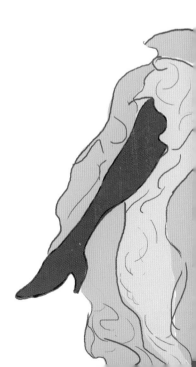

Raïto
Red wine and walnut sauce

Serves 4

This ancient sauce is believed to have originated in Greece but is now found mainly in Provence. Serve it hot with grilled or fried fish. It's also excellent with grilled lamb.

4 TABLESPOONS OLIVE OIL

2 SHALLOTS (ESCHALOTS), CHOPPED

1 CLOVE GARLIC, CRUSHED

2 CUPS RED WINE

250G (9OZ) TOMATOES, SKINNED, DESEEDED AND CHOPPED

1 SPRIG OF THYME

1 SPRIG OF ROSEMARY

1 CLOVE

4 TABLESPOONS WALNUT PIECES, TOASTED

2 TABLESPOONS BLACK OLIVES, CHOPPED

1 TABLESPOON SMALL CAPERS

SALT AND PEPPER

Heat the olive oil in a saucepan. Add the shallot and garlic and sauté until golden. Add the wine, tomatoes, sprigs of thyme and rosemary and the clove. Bring to the boil and then reduce to a simmer. Cook uncovered for 1 hour until reduced by one half in volume. Discard the herbs.

Crush the walnuts finely and add to the sauce to thicken. Cook for a further 10 minutes. Stir through the olives and capers, then season and serve.

Sauce bordelaise
Red wine and bone marrow sauce

Serves 4

This rich red wine sauce from Bordeaux studded with buttery marrow is perfect with steaks and roasted beef.

2 SHALLOTS (ESCHALOTS), CHOPPED

I CARROT, CHOPPED

I CLOVE GARLIC, SLICED

250ML (8FL OZ/1 CUP) RED WINE

100ML (3½FL OZ) PORT

500ML (16FL OZ/2 CUPS) BEEF STOCK

50G (1¾OZ) BONE MARROW

2 TEASPOONS CHOPPED PARSLEY

SALT AND PEPPER

Combine the shallots, carrot and garlic with the wine and port in a saucepan. Bring to the boil and reduce to a quarter of the original volume.

Pass the sauce through a sieve and discard the vegetables. Return the sauce to the pan and add the stock. Reduce by half, then season to taste.

Cut the marrow into thin slices and poach gently in boiling water. Drain the marrow, then add to the sauce along with the parsley. Check seasoning and serve.

Sauce diable
Devilled sauce

Serves 4

A devilishly good sauce, this cuts the richness of offal.

3 SHALLOTS (ESCHALOTS), CHOPPED
1 TABLESPOON BLACK PEPPERCORNS, CRUSHED
125ML (4FL OZ/½ CUP) WHITE WINE
2 TABLESPOONS RED WINE VINEGAR
500ML (16FL OZ/2 CUPS) BEEF STOCK
1 TEASPOON WORCESTERSHIRE SAUCE
1 TEASPOON DIJON MUSTARD
PINCH OF CAYENNE PEPPER
SALT

Combine the shallots, peppercorns, wine and vinegar in a saucepan. Bring to the boil and reduce until all the liquid has evaporated.

Add the stock and reduce by half. Stir in the Worcestershire sauce, mustard and cayenne. Adjust seasoning and serve.

Sauce poivrade
Pepper sauce

Serves 4

The classic sauce doesn't contain any cream. I add it so the pepperiness is revealed gradually.

55G (2OZ) BACON, CUT INTO THICK STRIPS

1 CARROT, CHOPPED

1 ONION, CHOPPED

1 TABLESPOON BLACK PEPPERCORNS, CRUSHED

4 TABLESPOONS COGNAC

1 TABLESPOON WHITE WINE VINEGAR

500ML (9FL OZ/2 CUPS) BEEF STOCK

125ML (4FL OZ/½ CUP) CREAM

2 TABLESPOONS GREEN PEPPERCORNS, CANNED

SALT

Place the bacon in a saucepan and cook until all the fat has rendered off and the strips are crisp and golden. Add the carrot, onion and black peppercorns and cook until the vegetables are caramelised.

Pour in the cognac and flambé by lighting; stand back and wait until the flames have subsided. Add the vinegar and stock, bring to the boil and reduce by half. Pass the sauce through a sieve, then add the cream and green peppercorns. Season to taste.

Soupes
Soups

Soupe à l'oignon gratinée
Caramelised onion soup with Gruyère croutons

Serves 4–6

A dish born in the famed Les Halles markets, once known as 'the stomach of Paris'. The Swiss Army knife of soups, it's a nourishing lunch, satisfying entrée or, as the French prefer, a late-night comforter. This classic has only a few ingredients, but its success lies in the correct caramelisation of the onions and the quality of the stock. Try to find the true Gruyère made in Switzerland to A. requirements.

60G (2OZ) BUTTER

10 BROWN ONIONS, FINELY SLICED

1 TEASPOON SALT

75G (2½ OZ) PLAIN FLOUR

2 LITRES (64FL OZ) BROWN BEEF
   STOCK (SEE RECIPE, PAGE 11)

1 BAY LEAF

½ BUNCH THYME

2 TABLESPOONS PARSLEY, CHOPPED

12 BAGUETTE CROUTONS

100G (3 ½ OZ) GRUYÈRE, CUT INTO
   12 SLICES

SALT AND PEPPER

Gently melt the butter in a heavy-based saucepan, add onions and 1 teaspoon of salt (the salt will draw out the juices of the onions, aiding the caramelisation process). Continue cooking uncovered on a medium low heat, stirring occasionally until the onions are mahogany coloured. This will take around 45 minutes. Even, slow cooking produces a sweet nutty flavour.

Sprinkle in the flour, stirring vigorously to avoid lumps and continue cooking for 2 minutes to cook out the raw flour taste. Add the hot stock gradually, stirring all the time. Tie the bay leaf and thyme in muslin and add to the soup. Lower the heat to a gentle simmer and cook uncovered for 30 minutes.

Remove the herbs and correct the seasoning. Pour into ovenproof soup tureens, float on a layer of croutons then the sliced cheese. Brown under a hot grill and sprinkle with chopped parsley. Serve immediately.

Soupe de poissons
Provençal fish soup

Serves 4–6

Versions of this soup are made up and down the Mediterranean coast. It is flavoured much like the famous bouillabaisse, the major difference being that the fish is pureed rather than served whole. Use this recipe just as guide, and customise the soup the way you like—for instance, you could replace the wine with Noilly Prat or a good slug of pastis. Just remember to keep the soup light and fragrant, it should not be overly fishy.

1KG (2LB 4OZ) WHOLE ROCKFISH
60ML (2FL OZ/¼ CUP) OLIVE OIL
2 ONIONS, CHOPPED
1 FENNEL BULB, TRIMMED AND
    CHOPPED
2 CELERY STICKS, TRIMMED AND
    CHOPPED
6 CLOVES GARLIC, CHOPPED
500G (17½OZ) TOMATOES, PEELED,
    SEEDED AND QUARTERED
125ML (4FL OZ/½ CUP) WHITE WINE

1 PINCH SAFFRON THREADS
½ TABLESPOON ORANGE ZEST
1 BAY LEAF
½ BUNCH THYME
¼ TEASPOON CAYENNE PEPPER
SALT AND PEPPER

TO SERVE
ROUILLE (SEE RECIPE, PAGE 13)
CROUTONS
GRATED PARMESAN

Wash the fish, scale and discard the fins. If the fish is large, cut it into smaller pieces.

Heat the olive oil in a large saucepan, then add the onions, fennel, celery and garlic. Cook gently, not allowing the vegetables to colour. Add the tomatoes, fish and wine. Top up with 1.5 litres (48fl oz/6 cups) of water, then add the saffron, orange zest, bay leaf, thyme, cayenne and a little seasoning (use about ½ teaspoon of salt). Bring to the boil, then simmer uncovered for 45 minutes.

Strain the soup through a sieve, then return the liquid to the pot. Puree the vegetables and fish in a food processor, then work the puree through a sieve. Add the puree to the reserved liquid and bring back to the boil. Adjust the seasoning. Serve hot with rouille, croutons and grated parmesan.

Crème vichyssoise glacée
Chilled leek and potato soup

Serves 4

Louis Diat, the creator of this famous soup and head chef of the Ritz-Carlton in New York, was one of the chefs credited with popularising French cuisine in the United States. In 1917, before air conditioning, hotel guests were entertained in the hotel's rooftop garden on balmy summer nights. Diat decided that a chilled soup would be the thing to serve them and he adapted the simple leek and potato soup his mother used to serve in their Bourbonnais home near the famous spa of Vichy.

2 LEEKS, WHITE PART ONLY, WASHED AND TRIMMED

1 TABLESPOON BUTTER

1 SMALL ONION, CHOPPED

2 MEDIUM POTATOES, PEELED AND CHOPPED

330ML (1⅓ CUP) WATER

500ML (16FL OZ/2 CUPS) MILK

250ML (8FL OZ/1 CUP) CREAM

SALT AND PEPPER

1 TABLESPOON CHIVES, CHOPPED

Slice the leeks finely. In a heavy-bottomed saucepan, melt the butter and add the leeks and onion. Cover and over a low heat, gently cook until soft and translucent. Add the potatoes and water and cook until the potatoes are tender. Transfer the soup to a blender and liquidise. Return the puree to the pot and add the milk. Bring back to the boil and then pass the soup through a fine mesh sieve. Cool, stirring occasionally so a skin does not form.

When cold, add the cream and pass through the sieve again. Cover, and chill in the fridge. Before serving, check the seasoning and mix well. Serve in chilled bowls and garnish with chopped chives.

Bisque de homard
Lobster bisque

Serves 4

This soup has all of the richness and flavour of lobster without the expense. All that is needed are the lobster heads, which have an extraordinary amount of flavour and also contain the highly prized 'tomalley' liver and roe.

30G (1OZ) BUTTER

1 CARROT, CHOPPED

1 ONION, CHOPPED

1 STICK CELERY, CHOPPED

250G (9OZ) LOBSTER HEADS

2 TABLESPOONS COGNAC

4 TOMATOES, CHOPPED

500ML (16FL OZ/2 CUPS) CHICKEN
   STOCK

125ML (4FL OZ/½ CUP) WHITE WINE

PINCH OF CAYENNE

PINCH OF NUTMEG

1 TEASPOON CORIANDER SEEDS

6 PEPPERCORNS

1 BAY LEAF

250ML (8FL OZ/1 CUP) CREAM

SALT AND PEPPER

Melt the butter in a frying pan. Add the carrot, onion and celery. Sauté until golden, then transfer to a saucepan. Cut the lobster heads into small pieces. Add to the frying pan and cook over a high heat until they turn bright red and fragrant. Pour in the cognac and flambé by lighting; stand back and wait until the flames have subsided.

Add the lobster to the saucepan with the sautéed vegetables and the tomatoes. Pour in the stock and wine along with the spices and bay leaf. Bring to the boil and simmer for 1 hour. Blend in a liquidiser. Pass through a fine sieve and return to a clean saucepan.

Bring back to the boil, then add cream. Adjust the seasoning and serve with a swirl of cream.

Crème du Barry
Cauliflower soup

Serves 4

Du Barry refers to dishes that have cauliflower as the predominant ingredient—they are named in honour of the Comtesse du Barry, aristocrat and the last mistress of Louis XV. This velvety soup goes particularly well with smoked fish or roe—try it garnished with smoked eel.

30G (1OZ) BUTTER

1 LEEK, SLICED

4 GARLIC CLOVES, CHOPPED

½ TEASPOON FENUGREEK SEEDS

½ HEAD CAULIFLOWER, CHOPPED

500ML (16FL OZ/2 CUPS) CHICKEN
  STOCK OR WATER

1 POTATO, CUBED

1 OIGNON CLOUTE (SEE PAGE 236)

250ML (8FL OZ/1 CUP) CREAM

PINCH OF NUTMEG

1 TABLESPOON PARSLEY, CHOPPED

SALT AND PEPPER

Melt the butter in a casserole and add the leek, garlic and fenugreek. Cook without colouring. Add the cauliflower, stock, potato and oignon cloute. Bring to the boil and simmer for 1 hour. Discard the oignon cloute. Process in a liquidiser until smooth, then pass through a fine sieve. Add the cream, nutmeg and seasoning. Reheat gently—don't boil. Sprinkle with parsley and serve.

Cressoniere
Creamed watercress soup

Serves 4

To make this soup a vibrant emerald green the watercress leaves are blended into the liquid at the last moment—they will cook in the hot soup. Choose small young watercress, as it tends to be bitter when older.

2 BUNCHES WATERCRESS

30G (1OZ) BUTTER

1 LEEK, SLICED

2 CLOVES GARLIC, CRUSHED

1 POTATO, SLICED

1 LITRE (36FL OZ/4 CUPS) CHICKEN STOCK OR WATER

200ML (7FL OZ/¾ CUP) CREAM OR CRÈME FRAÎCHE

SALT AND PEPPER

Wash the watercress thoroughly. Pick all the tender leaves from the stalks and set aside separately.

Melt the butter over low heat, then add the leek and garlic. Cook without colouring. Add the potato, watercress stalks and the stock. Bring to the boil and then simmer for 45 minutes.

Blend the soup in a liquidiser along with the reserved watercress leaves.

Return to the saucepan, add the cream and bring back to simmer—don't allow it to boil. Serve immediately with a drizzle of cream or crème fraîche.

Potage purée Saint-Germain
Pea pod and lettuce soup

Serves 4

This soup makes good use of otherwise wasted pea pods. Use frozen peas or mangetout if fresh peas are unavailable, but the finished soup will lack the intense grassy notes of pods. Saint-Germain in Paris was once a town well known for its pea production.

4 TABLESPOONS OLIVE OIL

I LEEK, SLICED

4 SHALLOTS (ESCHALOTS), CHOPPED

4 CLOVES GARLIC, SLICED

¼ TEASPOON NUTMEG

2 SPRIGS OF THYME

I OIGNON CLOUTE (SEE PAGE 236)

750ML (24FL OZ/3 CUPS) CHICKEN
  STOCK OR WATER

IKG (2LB 4OZ) PEAS, PODS ONLY,
  OR 500G (17½OZ) FROZEN PEAS

I HEAD BABY COS, SHREDDED

125ML (4FL OZ/½ CUP) CREAM

SALT AND PEPPER

4 TABLESPOONS CRÈME FRAÎCHE

4 SPRIGS OF CHERVIL

Heat the oil in a saucepan, then add the leek, shallots, garlic and nutmeg. Cook gently without colouring, then add the nutmeg, thyme, oignon cloute and stock. Bring to the boil, and simmer, covered, for 15 minutes. Add in the pea pods and cook for a further 15 minutes.

Discard the oignon cloute. Process the soup in a liquidiser, in batches, with the lettuce. Pass through a fine sieve and return to a clean saucepan. Pour in the cream and return to the heat—don't allow it to boil.

Adjust the seasoning. Pour into serving bowls, top with a spoon of crème fraîche and sprinkle over the chervil.

Soupe aux huîtres
Creamed oyster soup with samphire

Serves 4

Samphire is a plant that grows in coastal areas and has a pronounced salty sea flavour. This soup is also great chilled. If samphire is unavailable, sorrel is a good substitute.

30G (1OZ) BUTTER

1 LEEK, SLICED

2 CLOVES GARLIC

½ TEASPOON FENNEL SEEDS

½ TEASPOON CORIANDER SEEDS

125ML (4FL OZ/½ CUP) NOILLY
   PRAT OR OTHER FRENCH
   VERMOUTH

½ CELERIAC BULB, CHOPPED

1 OIGNON CLOUTE (SEE PAGE 236)

500ML (16FL OZ/2 CUPS) FISH OR
   CHICKEN STOCK

2 DOZEN OYSTERS, FRESHLY
   SHUCKED

250ML (4FL OZ/1 CUP) CREAM

SALT AND PEPPER

30G (1OZ) SAMPHIRE, BLANCHED

Melt the butter in a saucepan and add the leek, garlic and fennel and coriander seeds. Cook without colouring. Add the vermouth, celeriac, oignon cloute and stock and simmer, covered, for 45 minutes.

Discard the oignon cloute. Process in a liquidiser with 16 of the oysters. Pass through a fine sieve. Add the cream and bring back to a simmer.

Season to taste. Pour into warmed bowls. Garnish with the reserved oysters and the samphire.

Soupe à l'ail
Roasted garlic soup

Serves 4

Roasting the garlic mellows this otherwise pungent vegetable.

4 HEADS GARLIC
125ML (4FL OZ/½ CUP) OLIVE OIL
1 TABLESPOON FLOUR
1 LITRE (36FL OZ/4 CUPS) CHICKEN STOCK OR WATER
½ BUNCH THYME
55G (2OZ) VERMICELLI PASTA
½ BAGUETTE
1 TABLESPOON PARSLEY, CHOPPED
SALT AND PEPPER

Preheat the oven to 180°C (350°F). Cut the garlic heads in half through the centre—don't remove the skins. Place them cut side down in a casserole and pour over the oil. Bake in the heated oven for about 1 hour, until soft and golden. Squeeze out the roasted garlic flesh and discard the skins. Reserve the flesh from one of the heads of garlic separately.

Transfer the casserole to the stove top and on a low heat mash the garlic with a wooden spoon. Sprinkle in the flour and cook for a few minutes. Pour in the hot stock or water a little at a time, stirring constantly to ensure against lumps. Add the thyme and bring to the boil. Simmer, covered, for 30 minutes.

Add in the pasta and cook for a further 15 minutes. Adjust the seasoning.

Cut the baguette into thick slices and drizzle with a little olive oil. Toast in the oven until crisped and golden. Spread with the reserved garlic puree and place in centre of warmed serving bowls, then pour over the hot soup, adjust the seasoning, sprinkle with the parsley and serve immediately.

Soupe aux tomates rôties
Roasted tomato soup

Serves 4

This soup is the pure essence of tomatoes and does not have any liquid other than from the tomatoes. To be really successful, the tomatoes need to be plump and juicy. Serve with toast spread with tapenade.

1.5KG (3LB 5OZ) TOMATOES, HALVED	4 TABLESPOONS OLIVE OIL
2 ONIONS, CHOPPED	1 TABLESPOON BROWN SUGAR
8 CLOVES GARLIC, SLICED	1 TEASPOON SMOKED PAPRIKA
½ BUNCH THYME	½ TEASPOON CORIANDER SEED
½ BUNCH BASIL	½ TEASPOON CUMIN SEED
2 TABLESPOONS BALSAMIC VINEGAR	SALT AND PEPPER

Preheat the oven to 200°C (400°F). Combine all the ingredients except the seasoning in a bowl. Mix well. Spread on a deep roasting tray and roast in the hot oven for about 1 hour, until the tomatoes are well coloured and collapsed.

Pass through a mouli into a saucepan. Bring to a simmer, then adjust the seasoning.

Entrées

Soufflé au fromage
Twice-baked cheese soufflé

Serves 4

This soufflé has two advantages over the traditional one. It can be prepared in advance and isn't notoriously temperamental. This recipe is successful with other cheeses—try a soft chevre or Roquefort. Ovenproof dariole moulds work well and so do teacups!

370 ML (13FL OZ/1½ CUP) MILK
80G (2½OZ) BUTTER
60G (2OZ) FLOUR
100G (3½OZ) GRUYÈRE, GRATED
3 EGGS, SEPARATED, PLUS 1 EGG
  WHITE

FRESHLY GRATED NUTMEG
SALT AND PEPPER
300ML (10FL OZ/1¼ CUP) CREAM
4 TABLESPOONS GRATED PARMESAN

Preheat the oven to 180°C (350°F). Heat the milk (don't boil it) in a small saucepan. In a another saucepan melt the butter, then add the flour and cook gently on low heat for 3 minutes. Pour in the hot milk and stir vigorously until you have a smooth glossy sauce. Continue to cook for 5 minutes, stirring all the time.

Take the pan from the heat, stir in the cheese until it is melted and smooth; cool. Transfer the sauce to a large bowl, add the egg yolks and mix well. Add a little freshly grated nutmeg and season well. Whisk the egg whites until soft peaks form. Gently fold a third of the whites through the sauce to lighten the mix. Then add the rest of the whites and fold through until you have a smooth homogenous mix.

Pour into individual moulds, which have been buttered and floured well. Place in a bain-marie and bake in the heated oven for about 35 minutes, until the soufflés have risen, are lightly browned and a skewer comes out clean when inserted into the centres. Cool completely. Invert the moulds to remove the soufflés.

At this stage the soufflés can be kept refrigerated for up to three days until needed. To serve, preheat the oven to 200°C (400°F). Place the soufflés in ovenproof gratin dishes, pour over the cream, sprinkle over the parmesan and season. Bake for 15 minutes, until puffed and golden brown. Serve immediately.

Omelette aux champignons
Mushroom omelette

For 1 omelette

Eggs are one of nature's super foods, packaged conveniently in a shell. Their versatility makes them indispensable in the bistro kitchen, where they are used in all aspects of the menu—hors d'oeuvres, salads, mains and practically all desserts.

An omelette can be a light starter or a complete meal, depending on the choice of filling—and time of day. Always use super-fresh eggs and never add milk, which will toughen the omelette. Instead, add a little water to give a light fluffy result. This recipe uses regular button mushrooms for ease of availability, but of course you can substitute exotic varieties when in season. For a special touch, shave over some fresh truffle or drizzle with truffled oil.

60G (2OZ) BUTTER
150G (5OZ) BUTTON MUSHROOMS, SLICED
3 EGGS
1 TABLESPOON WATER
CHIVES TO GARNISH
SALT AND PEPPER

In a 20-cm (8-in) omelette pan, heat half the butter. Add the mushrooms and sauté for a couple of minutes until softened and coloured. Season and set aside. Clean the pan.

Whisk together the eggs and water with a little seasoning. Melt the remaining butter in the omelette pan. Cook until the butter sizzles but not colours. Pour in the egg mixture and, using a fork, gently stir so that the eggs cook evenly without colouring.

Once the eggs have almost set, arrange the mushrooms in the centre. Fold over one third of the omelette to cover the mushrooms. Then tip the pan to 45 degrees so that the omelette slides to the edge of the pan. Fold over another third of the omelette. Flip the pan upside down onto a plate. You should have a perfectly formed omelette with the mushrooms encased. Garnish with chives and serve immediately.

Brandade de morue
Salt cod and potato puree

Serves 4

This may not sound like the most appealing of dishes but, believe me, it is terribly morish, almost addictive. Salt cod has a smoky quality and a strong fish flavour compared with fresh cod. This means that is usually paired with equally robust ingredients. Choose a strong, grassy extra virgin olive oil to stand up to the fish.

To obtain a smooth emulsion, the fish, milk and potato all need to be hot. Leftover brandade may be moulded into croquettes, then crumbed and deep-fried, and served with tomato sauce and crisp salad leaves.

500G (17½OZ) SALT COD
BOUQUET GARNI
160 ML (5½FL OZ/⅔ CUP) MILK
1 GARLIC CLOVE, CRUSHED
185ML (6FL OZ/¾ CUP) EXTRA
  VIRGIN OLIVE OIL

1 POTATO, BAKED SKIN ON
TOAST FOR SERVNG
GREEN OLIVES FOR SERVING

Soak the cod for 24 hours or up to 48 hours, changing the water several times. Place the fish and bouquet garni in a large pot and cover with water. Poach on a low heat for 10 minutes. Do not boil—this will turn the fish tough and stringy. Discard the bouquet garni, drain and let cool slightly.

Remove the skin and bones and flake the fish into a food processor. Scald the milk. Blend briefly to roughly cut up the fish, then add the garlic and scalded milk. Blend to incorporate and, with the motor running, drizzle in the olive oil as if you were making mayonnaise. Once you have a thick smooth emulsion, add the scooped out flesh of the potato. Pulse to mix through—do not blend for long or the potato will turn the mix waxy. Serve at room temperature with toast rubbed with garlic and green olives.

Croque monsieur
Toasted ham and cheese sandwich

Serves 4

This is the meat pie of France. It is quick, simple and satisfying. Use the best ham you can find, top-quality bread, a cheese such as Comte with a lingering sweet grassy note, and let the butter become nutty brown for enhanced depth of flavour. Add a fried egg on top and you have a croque madame for a more substantial meal.

8 SLICES WHITE BREAD
100G (3½OZ) COMTE OR GRUYÈRE CHEESE, CUT INTO 8 SLICES
4 SLICES HAM
200G (7OZ) BUTTER
BUTCHERS' TWINE

Lay out four of the bread slices and top each with a slice of cheese. Then lay a piece of ham on each. Top with cheese and then the bread to make the sandwich.

Generously butter the sandwiches on both the outer sides. Tie each sandwich crossways with the string to secure. Heat a frying pan to medium and cook until crisp and golden. Turn and repeat on the other side.

Remove the string and serve.

Cervelles d'agneau
Lambs' brains fritters

Serves 4

I have included this recipe because lambs' brains still have quite a following. The traditional way of serving this dish is to poach the brains and then serve in a butter flavoured with capers, lemon and parsley butter, much like à la meunière. I prefer them crumbed and deep fried. Think of them as the most luscious chicken nuggets you will ever taste. I like to serve the brains with a celeriac remoulade, which is simply freshly grated celeriac mixed through remoulade sauce (see recipe, page 14).

4 LAMB'S BRAINS

1 ONION, CHOPPED

1 CARROT, CHOPPED

JUICE OF 1 LEMON

BOUQUET GARNI

2 EGGS

125ML (4FL OZ/½ CUP) MILK

100G (3½OZ) SEASONED FLOUR

200G (7OZ) BREADCRUMBS

VEGETABLE OIL FOR DEEP-FRYING

SALT AND PEPPER

Soak the brains in lightly salted cold water for a few hours or overnight, to draw out any blood. Drain and rinse, then trim off any membranes.

To prepare the poaching liquid for the brains, pour 1 litre (36fl oz) of water into a saucepan with the onion, carrot, lemon juice and bouquet garni; bring to the boil, then cool. Put the prepared brains into a saucepan and strain the cooled liquid over them. Bring to a gentle simmer uncovered and cook for about 10 minutes. Remove the brains from the liquid and dry on paper towels. Cool and put into the fridge until they are completely cold.

In a bowl whisk together the eggs and milk. Dredge the brains in the seasoned flour, then dust off the excess; dip into the egg mixture and finally coat in breadcrumbs. Deep-fry at 180°C (350°F) until golden brown. Drain on paper towels and season.

Os à la moelle persillade
Roast marrow bone with parsley puree

Serves 4

This dish brings a touch of theatre to the table, in an interactive way. Bone marrow is available from all good butchers, who will cut it for you. Try to use French gros sel, coarse sea salt, which is less salty than regular salt and is not to be confused with rock salt, which is worlds away. Its large crystals add crunch to the dish. Give your guests small spoons in which to scoop out the intensely beef-flavoured fatty goodness. You needn't worry because marrow is known to maintain healthy cholesterol levels.

4 BEEF MARROW BONES, CUT INTO
5-CM (2-IN) PIECES
1 BUNCH PARSLEY
1 CLOVE GARLIC, CRUSHED
2 TABLESPOONS OLIVE OIL

1 BAGUETTE, SLICED AND TOASTED
WHITE PEPPER
GROS SEL
SALT AND PEPPER

Scrape down the bones to remove any meat or sinew. Submerge in lightly salted water for a few hours to draw out any blood. At this stage the marrow bones can be roasted or left over night.

To make the parsley puree, pick all the leaves from the parsley and plunge into salted boiling water for 10 seconds. Immediately drain and put into iced water. This process will 'set' the colour. Drain the parsley well, and squeeze it in a tea towel to extract all moisture. Place the parsley in a blender with the crushed garlic and a little salt and pepper. Blend with the oil until you have a smooth vibrant green puree. Store, covered, in the fridge.

Preheat the oven to 180°C (350°F). Remove the bones from the water and rinse, then dry throughly. Roast in the oven for 20 minutes. Carefully transfer the bones to serving plates and place a demitasse spoon into the top of each. Serve the parsley puree, toasted baguette and salt on the side.

Melon jambon
Charentais melon with ham and port

Serves 4

This simple hors d'oeuvre relies on the finest quality ham and the melon to be at the peak of condition. Bayonne ham, which is commonly used, is dry cured for 12 months. It is not widely available outside France, so the Italian prosciutto di parma is a good substitute. For the ultimate in ham, try the Spanish jamon iberico, which is made from black pigs fed almost exclusively on acorns, then cured for up to three years.

½ ROCK OR CHARENTAIS MELON
200G (7OZ) CURED, AIR-DRIED HAM, CUT WAFER THIN
2 TABLESPOONS PORT
BLACK PEPPER

Peel and deseed the melon. Cut into 12 wedges. Drizzle with the port and leave to macerate for 15 minutes. Arrange the melon on a platter and drape over the ham slices. Season with pepper.

Huîtres mignonette
Oysters with black pepper and shallot vinegar

Serves 2–4

Casanova was said to have consumed 60 of these a day. However, there is no evidence of aphrodisiac-giving qualities in oysters. Maybe it's the primal act of swallowing a live creature whole that is more of a turn on?

Oysters, as with other shellfish, require the least amount of effort to get the best result. Simply freshly shucked and served with lemon or flavoured vinegar is enough. You may also accompany them with buttered bread, as the butter extends the flavour.

Do try your hand at opening your own oysters—it's the only way to ensure freshness and not lose any of the briny juices.

24 OYSTERS
LEMON WEDGES TO SERVE

MIGNONETTE SAUCE
1 SHALLOT (ESCHALOT), FINELY CHOPPED
6 TABLESPOONS RED WINE VINEGAR
1 TEASPOON BLACK PEPPER, COARSELY GROUND

Mix the shallot with the vinegar, add the pepper and refrigerate to develop the flavour until needed.

Serve the oysters on a large platter of crushed ice, accompanied with the sauce and lemon wedges separately. Serve with the bottom muscle uncut and the top shell replaced. This displays the oysters in their beautiful entirety and shows your guests that they are fresh.

Saumon marine à l'aneth
Dill-cured salmon (gravlax)

Serves 8

This dish is borrowed from Scandinavia, where it is commonly known as gravlax. This was originally a method to preserve the salmon over the harsh winter months. The salmon was salted, covered in pine needles and buried in the sand above the high-tide line—'grav' means grave and 'lax' is salmon. This was replaced by this fresh sweet herbaceous method. You need to start this dish two days in advance, but once cured the salmon will keep for a week.

I SALMON FILLET, DEBONED, WITH SKIN ON

3 TABLESPOONS DILL, CHOPPED

SALT CURE

180G (6OZ) ROCK SALT

350G (12OZ) SUGAR

I TABLESPOON MUSTARD SEEDS

I TABLESPOON CORIANDER SEEDS

I BUNCH DILL

3 TABLESPOONS PASTIS

Combine all the cure ingredients in a food processor or blender and blend until you have a green paste. Spread the paste over both sides of the salmon and refrigerate, skin side down, overnight.

The following day, turn the salmon over and return to the fridge for a day.

Rinse the salmon throughly under cold running water and pat dry. Scatter the freshly chopped dill over the flesh side of the salmon and wrap tightly in plastic. Refrigerate until needed.

Serve it finely sliced on rye bread with crème fraîche and salmon roe as an hors d'oeuvre or drape large slices over a beetroot and fennel salad with citrus vinaigrette for something more substantial.

Poireaux vinaigrette
Marinated leeks with chopped eggs

Serves 4

Although they are often called poor man's asparagus, leeks are the kings of the onion family. This dish is a classic cold hors d'oeuvre served as an appetiser. I like to eat it slightly warmed with a poached egg and a scattering of fried forest mushrooms for lunch or as an elegant starter.

8 SMALL LEEKS
500ML (16FL OZ/2 CUPS) WHITE
    WINE
1 TABLESPOON WHOLEGRAIN
    MUSTARD
3 TABLESPOONS WHITE WINE
    VINEGAR
4 TABLESPOONS OLIVE OIL

8 CORIANDER SEEDS
1 BAY LEAF
½ BUNCH THYME
SALT AND WHITE PEPPER
2 EGGS, HARD-BOILED AND ROUGHLY
    CHOPPED
2 TABLESPOONS PARSLEY, CHOPPED

Trim the green part and the roots from the leeks. Wash throughly to remove any grit. If small leeks are unavailable, use larger ones split in half lengthways. Be sure not to cut off too much of the root section or the leek will fall apart.

Place the leeks in a casserole. In a bowl, combine 250ml (9fl oz/1 cup) water with the wine, mustard, vinegar, olive oil, coriander seeds, bay leaf, thyme and seasoning; pour over the leeks. Cover and simmer on top of the stove for 15–20 minutes, until the leeks are tender. Remove the leeks and set aside. Strain the remaining liquid through a sieve into a small saucepan; place over heat and reduce by half. Return the leeks to the liquid and chill.

To serve, transfer the leeks to serving plates or a platter and dress with a little of the marinade. Scatter over the chopped eggs and parsley.

Coquilles Saint-Jacques antiboise
Scallops with roast tomatoes, olives and basil

Serves 4

'Antiboise' refers to dishes cooked in the manner of the Provençal city of Antibes. Freshly opened scallops should be used. They are cooked briefly under a hot grill in their shells— this heats the shell, producing a more pronounced flavour of the sea and it gently warms the dressing, helping the flavours to meld together and release their aromas.

I CUP ROCK SALT

I2 CHERRY TOMATOES

I TABLESPOON SMALL BLACK OLIVES,
    PITTED AND DICED

I TABLESPOON GREEN OLIVES,
    PITTED AND DICED

I CLOVE GARLIC, FINELY SLICED

I SHALLOT (ESCHALOT), CHOPPED

4 ANCHOVY FILLETS, CUT INTO FINE
    STRIPS

I TABLESPOON LILLIPUT CAPERS

4 BASIL LEAVES, FINELY SHREDDED

75ML (2½FL OZ/⅓ CUP) OLIVE OIL

JUICE OF I LEMON

I2 SCALLOPS

Preheat the oven to 180°C (350°F). Spread the rock salt onto an oven tray. Place the tomatoes on top. Bake for 15–20 minutes until slightly blistered. Set the tomatoes aside.

To make the dressing, combine all the remaining ingredients except the scallops. Stir well to combine.

In the same tray used for the tomatoes arrange the scallops in their half shells on the rock salt. Place under a hot grill for 1–2 minutes until they just turn opaque.

Transfer to serving plates with small mounds of rock salt on which to steady the shells underneath. Top each scallop with a tomato. Spoon over some dressing and serve immediately.

Tartare de thon rouge, avocat et tomates

Red tuna with tomatoes and avocado cream

Serves 4

Only the freshest sushi-grade tuna should be used for this recipe. This is paramount—the other ingredients are added simply as seasonings to enhance the tuna. Other oily fish—such as kingfish and salmon, or even mackerel—also work well with the recipe.

400G (14OZ) TUNA

2 TOMATOES

½ AVOCADO

2 TABLESPOONS CRÈME FRAÎCHE

JUICE OF ½ LEMON

1 SHALLOT (ESCHALOT), FINELY DICED

1 TABLESPOON CORNICHONS

1 ANCHOVY FILLET, FINELY CHOPPED

1 TABLESPOON OLIVE OIL

½ BUNCH CHIVES

SALT AND FRESHLY GROUND BLACK PEPPER

Cut the tuna into small 5-mm (¼-in) dice. Cover and put in the fridge to chill.

Plunge the tomatoes into boiling water for 5 seconds and then straight into iced water. Peel and cut into quarters lengthways. Remove the stem and seeds, discard. Cut the tomato flesh into the same size dice as the tuna. Chill in the fridge.

Prepare the sauce by forcing the avocado flesh through a fine sieve into a bowl. Add the crème fraîche and lemon juice. Mix well. Season.

To serve, mix the tuna with the tomatoes, the shallot, cornichons and anchovy. Season if necessary. Place a ring mould on a serving plate and gently pack in the tuna; remove the mould. Add a dollop of the avocado sauce to the side. Garnish with chives and a drizzle of olive oil.

Parfait de foies de volaille
Chicken liver parfait with Armagnac butter

Serves 8–10

This is a finer texture than pâté and more spreadable. It can be cooked and served in any dish you like, covered with a port jelly or natural. I serve it encased in an Armagnac-scented butter for extra richness and depth. You could also shave over black truffle!

1KG (2LB 4OZ) CHICKEN LIVERS
6 SHALLOTS (ESCHALOTS), CHOPPED
6 CLOVES GARLIC, CRUSHED
1 BAY LEAF
½ BUNCH THYME
160ML (5½FL OZ/⅔ CUP) PORT
350G (12OZ) BUTTER, AT ROOM
  TEMPERATURE

250ML (8FL OZ/1 CUP) CREAM
3 EGG YOLKS
⅛ TEASPOON SALTPETRE
SALT AND BLACK PEPPER

ARMAGNAC BUTTER
1 TABLESPOON ARMAGNAC
250G (9OZ) BUTTER, AT ROOM
  TEMPERATURE

Preheat the oven to 160°C (325°F). Pick over the livers, removing excess sinew. Place shallots, garlic, herbs and port in a saucepan and over a low heat reduce the liquid by half. Pass through a sieve. In a blender combine the chicken livers, butter, cream, egg yolks, saltpetre and the port reduction. Blend to a fine liquid and then pass through a fine mesh sieve. Season.

Line a terrine mould with plastic film. Pour the chicken liver mixture into the mould, cover, and place in a bain-marie; bake in oven for 1 hour. The mix will rise a little when done (75°C/150°F on a meat thermometer). Leave to chill in the fridge, preferably overnight.

Cover a cutting board with a sheet of greaseproof paper and carefully turn out the parfait onto it. Whip the butter and Armagnac together until light and white. Using a palate knife, spread the three exposed sides with a 5-mm (¼-in) thick layer of the butter (like icing a cake). Set in the fridge until the butter has hardened, then turn over and spread the fourth side with remaining butter. Refrigerate until the butter has hardened, then wrap the parfait in plastic film.

Serve in thick slices with cornichons and toasted bread or brioche.

Escargots à la bourguignonne
Baked snails with garlic and parsley butter

Serves 4

The French love affair with these gastropods shows no sign of slowing down and in fact most snails consumed in France are imported to meet the demand.

Canned snails are available at most good supermarkets and delis. Shells are a little harder to find—however, once you have them they can be washed and reused—alternatively, it's perfectly acceptable to serve the dish without them. Escargotiere are cooking dishes with small indentations to stop the snails rolling around and are readily available, as are special 'snail' forks and tongs. Of course, they are all expendable, but it is a ceremony that adds to this dish.

350G (12OZ) BUTTER

5 CLOVES GARLIC, CRUSHED

2 SHALLOTS (ESCHALOTS) CHOPPED

3 TABLESPOONS PARSLEY, CHOPPED

SALT AND PEPPER

4 DOZEN SNAILS, CANNED

4 DOZEN SNAIL SHELLS

BAGUETTE TO SERVE

Bring the butter to room temperature. Add the garlic, shallots, parsley and seasoning to the butter. Mix well, and transfer to a piping bag.

Drain the snails carefully and rinse under water; drain again. Pipe the garlic butter into the snail shells to half full. Place a snail on top and seal with more butter. At this stage, they can be kept in the fridge, covered, for a couple of days.

Preheat the oven to 180°C (350°F). Arrange the prepared snails in the cooking dishes, making sure that the openings are facing up. Cook in the heated oven for about 10 minutes, until the butter is bubbling hot. Serve with enough baguettes to mop up the butter and juices.

Pâté de campagne
Country-style terrine

Makes 1kg (2lb 4oz) terrine

The thought of making a terrine may be overwhelming. But essentially, it is a meatloaf, albeit a luxurious one. Pork liver, the predominant flavouring, gives the terrine its luscious buttery texture. A terrine is always served cold and is best eaten 48 hours after making. It will keep for up to a week.

There are an infinite variety of terrines, pâté de campagne being the most basic—it's often described as 'pâté maison' on bistro menus. The following is the basic recipe but you can customise it to make it your own. I like to add a handful of toasted pistachios or Armagnac-soaked prunes. Crepinette is the fatty net-like lining which holds pigs' intestines in place. It has a slight offally taste and when cooked melds into the terrine. You can replace it with slices of streaky bacon if desired.

Serve slices of the terrine with crusty baguette, some good Dijon mustard and cornichons. It forms an integral part of an 'assiette de charcuterie'—a platter of select pork charcuterie preparations, usually terrine, rillettes (see recipe, page 73), cured ham and saucisson sec— and is an excellent starter or luncheon dish with a crisp green salad and lots of bread.

400G (14OZ) PORK LIVER

1 TABLESPOON VEGETABLE OIL

2 TABLESPOONS COGNAC

30G (1OZ) BUTTER

4 SHALLOTS (ESCHALOTS), CHOPPED

1 CLOVE GARLIC, CHOPPED

1 BAY LEAF

1 TABLESPOON THYME LEAVES, CHOPPED

½ CUP BREADCRUMBS

125M (4FL OZ/½ CUP) CREAM

600G (1LB 5OZ) PORK SHOULDER

2 EGGS

1 TABLESPOON SALT

½ TEASPOON QUATRE ÉPICES

1 TEASPOON FRESHLY GROUND BLACK PEPPER

1 TABLESPOON CHOPPED PARSLEY

100G (2½OZ) CREPINETTE OR STREAKY BACON

Preheat the oven to 180°C (350°F).

Cut the liver into 2.5-cm (1-in) cubes. Heat the oil in a pan until smoking. Add the liver and cook briefly till browned. Pour in cognac and flambé by lighting; stand back and wait until the flames have subsided. Transfer to a bowl to cool.

Melt the butter in the same pan, add the shallots, garlic, bay leaf and thyme. Fry gently until fragrant and caramelised. Discard the bay leaf. Add the mixture to the liver.

Combine the breadcrumbs and cream. Leave to stand until the crumbs have plumped up.

Mince the pork shoulder through the large dice on a mincer. Then add the mince to the liver and mix thoroughly. Add in the breadcrumbs, eggs, seasonings and spices and the parsley. Mix thoroughly.

Line the terrine mould with the crepinette or bacon, leaving an overhang. Fill with the meat mix. Fold the crepinette over the top to encase the filling.

Place the terrine in a bain-marie filled with hot water. Bake in the preheated oven for about 1½ hours, until the juices run clear when a skewer is inserted. Leave to cool.

Turn out of the mould, wrap in plastic film and refrigerate for least 24 hours before use.

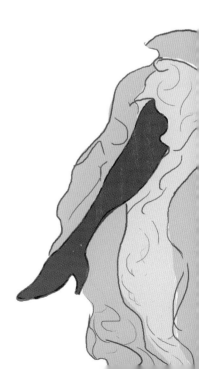

Rillettes de Tours
Potted pork terrine

Serves 4

Rillettes, a speciality of Loire, is a spreadable pork pâté. There are many different versions. In Le Mans they use half pork, half goose; elsewhere rabbit and pork are common. In Tours pure pork is preferred.

1 KG (2LB 4OZ) PORK BELLY, CUT INTO 5-CM (2-IN) CUBES, ON
   OR OFF THE BONE
1 TABLESPOON SALT
½ TEASPOON QUATRE ESPICE
1 BAY LEAF
250ML (8FL OZ/1 CUP) WATER
SALT AND PEPPER

Preheat the oven to 150°C (300°F). Place the pork in a casserole along with the salt, quatre espice, bay leaf and water. Also add the pork bones, if bought whole—this will intensify the flavour. Bring to the boil and place in the heated oven, covered, for 4–5 hours. Check occasionally that the meat hasn't stuck to the dish and top up with water if necessary. When all the fat is rendered and clear, it is ready.

Drain off the fat and reserve. Remove the bay leaf, and bones if used, and discard. Shred the pork, season to taste and pack into glass or earthenware serving dishes. Top with a layer of reserved fat and store, covered, in the fridge for up to two weeks. Serve at room temperature with cornichons, mustard and plenty of crusty bread.

Salades
Salads

Salade Niçoise
Niçoise salad

Serves 4

A speciality of Nice, this salad is the subject of many heated debates over the authenticity of ingredients. The 'modern' salade Niçoise is often a heavy jumble of cooked green beans, potatoes, assorted lettuces and oily vinaigrette. It's far removed from the salad's origins on the Cote d'Azur. The genuine recipe has the simplicity of nothing but raw vegetables, boiled eggs, canned tuna or anchovies in oil, and not even a dressing. If you are a purist by all means use only raw vegetables, but I find that cooked artichokes and broad beans are more palatable.

2 VINE-RIPENED TOMATOES, CUT INTO THICK SLICES

2 HARDBOILED EGGS

4 ARTICHOKE HEARTS, CANNED OR RAW

200G (7OZ) CANNED TUNA IN OIL

4 TABLESPOONS TAPENADE (SEE PAGE 16)

100G (3½OZ) BROAD BEANS, BOILED AND SKINNED OR RAW

4 ANCHOVY FILLETS, CUT INTO SLIVERS

2 SHALLOTS (ESCHALOTS), CHOPPED

4 TEASPOONS LILLIPUT CAPERS

30G (1OZ) BLACK OLIVES

4 LEAVES BASIL, SHREDDED

1 LEMON, CUT INTO WEDGES

Place 2 tomato slices, an artichoke heart and half an egg on each plate. Drain the tuna, but not throughly, as the oil will be part of the dressing component. Divide the tuna between the four plates and add a spoon of tapenade to each. Scatter over the remaining ingredients. Drizzle with the oil from the tuna or anchovy and garnish with a lemon wedge.

Salade catalane
Roasted fennel, capsicum, anchovy and egg salad

Serves 4

This is a great luncheon dish best served freshly made while the fennel and peppers are still warm and fragrant. Serve with crusty bread to mop up the juices.

1 RED OR YELLOW CAPSICUM
(BELL PEPPER)

2 FENNEL BULBS

4 TABLESPOONS OLIVE OIL

4 EGGS

1 CLOVE GARLIC, HALVED

2 TOMATOES, SLICED

8 ANCHOVY FILLETS

2 TABLESPOONS BLACK OLIVES,
PITTED AND CHOPPED

4 TABLESPOONS PARSLEY, SHREDDED

SALT AND PEPPER

Preheat the oven to 180°C (350°F). Remove the stems and seeds from the pepper and cut into thick slices. Slice the fennel thickly. Toss in the olive oil and roast in the heated oven for 45 minutes, until tender and slightly browned.

Boil the eggs in salted water for 10 minutes. Cool, remove shells and tear the eggs in half.

Rub the serving plates with the cut surface of the garlic. Arrange the sliced tomatoes, fennel and peppers on the places and season. Top with the egg and anchovy fillets. Scatter over the olives and parsley.

Salade de chèvre chaud
Grilled goat's cheese salad

Serves 4

For this salad I suggest you use bitter salad greens able to stand up to the goat's cheese. A French chèvre, of course, is ideal.

1 LARGE BEETROOT

1 TABLESPOON OLIVE OIL

1 TABLESPOON RED WINE VINEGAR

2 HEADS WITLOF, RED OR WHITE

1 HEAD FRISÉE (CURLY ENDIVE)

12 LEAVES RED OAK LETTUCE

12 SLICES OF BAGUETTE

1 CLOVE GARLIC, HALVED

200G (7OZ) CHEVRE, SLICED

2 SHALLOTS (ESCHALOTS), CHOPPED

90G (3OZ) WALNUT PIECES, TOASTED

6 TABLESPOONS WALNUT
   VINAIGRETTE (SEE PAGE 15)

Preheat the oven to 180°C (350°F). Throughly wash the beetroot and place on a square of aluminum foil. Drizzle with the olive oil and vinegar and bake in the heated oven for about 45 minutes, until tender. Peel while still warm, then cut into wedges.

Wash and dry the salad greens. Rub the baguette slices with the garlic. Place the bread on an oven tray with a slice of cheese on top of each. Grill until golden and bubbling. Immediately transfer to serving plates. Arrange the beetroot, greens, shallot and walnut pieces around the cheese. Drizzle with the vinaigrette and serve.

Salade frisée aux lardons
Warm salad of greens, bacon and poached eggs

Serves 4

Bacon and eggs are undoubtedly the world's favourite combination, so why not as a salad? Be sure to soft-poach the eggs—the molten yolk mixed through the leaves together with bacon-scented dressing becomes a wonderful homogenous mess.

2 HEADS FRISÉE (CURLY ENDIVE)

1 TABLESPOON WHITE WINE VINEGAR

4 EGGS

200G (7OZ) THICK FATTY BACON, CUT INTO LARDONS

2 SLICES COUNTRY-STYLE BREAD

1 TABLESPOON RED WINE VINEGAR

2 SHALLOTS (ESCHALOTS), CHOPPED

1 TEASPOON DIJON MUSTARD

1 TABLESPOON OLIVE OIL

SALT AND PEPPER

Wash the frisée heads and remove the dark tough leaves. Break the hearts into small fronds.

Boil 1 litre (1¾ pints) of water and add the white wine vinegar. Reduce to a simmer. Break the eggs into separate cups and gently slip each into the simmering water. Poach for 3 minutes. Remove the eggs with a slotted spoon and set aside.

Fry the lardons in a dry frying pan until crisp, golden and the fat has been rendered off. Remove the lardons with a slotted spoon and set aside. Do not clean the pan.

Cut the bread into 1-cm (½-in) cubes. Fry them in the bacon fat until golden. Remove and add to lardons.

Make a dressing by deglazing the pan with the red wine vinegar. Stir in the shallots, mustard and olive oil. Season to taste.

Toss the frisée with the dressing. Arrange on individual serving plates. Top each with an egg and scatter over the lardons and croutons. Serve immediately.

Salade Roquefort
Salad of witlof, pear, Roquefort and walnuts

Serves 4

This salad is a symphony of crisp bitter witlof, salty sharp roquefort, sweet pear and mealy walnuts. Serve as a side dish or entree.

2 HEADS WILTOF
1 PEAR, UNPEELED AND SLICED
60G (2OZ) WALNUT PIECES, TOASTED

ROQUEFORT DRESSING
1 SHALLOT (ESCHALOT), CHOPPED
1 TEASPOON DIJON MUSTARD

1 TABLESPOON WHITE WINE
  VINEGAR
3 TABLESPOONS WALNUT OIL
2 TABLESPOONS CRÈME FRAICHE
WHITE PEPPER
100G (3½OZ) ROQUEFORT

To make the dressing, combine all ingredients except the cheese. Break up the Roquefort, keeping it in largish chunks, and stir through the dressing. Season with pepper.

Separate the witlof leaves. Wash and dry. Toss through with the dressing. Arrange over the sliced pear, scatter over the walnuts and serve.

Salade landaise
Warm salad of duck breast and foie gras

Serves 4

The Landes, a region of Gascony in the southwest of France, is a major producer of foie gras. This salad combines all the best the duck has to offer. Confit duck gizzards are luscious little morsels, available canned at good delis.

200G (7OZ) CONFIT DUCK GIZZARDS

2 SHALLOTS (ESCHALOTS), CHOPPED

3 CUPS MIXED SALAD LEAVES

4 TABLESPOONS WALNUT
VINAIGRETTE (SEE RECIPE,
PAGE 15)

1 TOMATO, SLICED

1 X 200G (7OZ) SMOKED DUCK
MAGRET BREAST, SLICED

4 X 15G (½OZ) FOIE GRAS

2 TABLESPOONS WALNUTS PIECES,
TOASTED

SALT AND PEPPER

Fry the gizzards in a little of the fat they come packed in. Once crisp and golden, add the shallots. Continue to cook until shallots are caramelised. Set aside and keep warm.

Wash and thoroughly dry the salad leaves. Toss the salad leaves with the vinaigrette. Place the tomato slices on serving plates and top with the salad leaves, then the sliced duck magret and foie gras. Scatter over the gizzards, shallots and walnuts. Season to taste and serve immediately.

Pois chiches en salade
Chickpea and tuna salad

Serves 4

This is an unusual salad using an emulsified tuna dressing, which is used quite widely in the Mediterranean—perhaps most famously by the Italians in vitello tonnato, a cold veal dish with a similar tuna sauce.

In Provence, dried salted mullet roe, called poutarge, is grated over the salad to accentuate the subtle tuna flavour. However, it is quite difficult to find and very expensive. Anchovy fillets are a good substitute.

250G (9OZ) CHICKPEAS

125G (4OZ) TUNA, CANNED
   IN OLIVE OIL

1 CLOVE GARLIC

1 TEASPOON DIJON MUSTARD

125ML (4FL OZ/½ CUP) OLIVE OIL

2 TABLESPOONS LEMON JUICE

1 RED CAPSICUM (BELL PEPPER),
   SLICED

½ RED ONION, SLICED

1 TABLESPOON PARSLEY, CHOPPED

SALT AND PEPPER

Soak the chickpeas overnight or for a minimum of 8 hours. Rinse well and place in a saucepan, cover with cold water and bring to the boil. Simmer for about 1 hour, until tender. Drain in a colander and keep warm.

To make the dressing, drain the tuna well, reserving the oil. Place the tuna in a food processor along with the garlic and mustard. Blend well to obtain a smooth puree. In a thin stream add in the reserved tuna oil and olive oil. Continue to blend until you have a sauce of a thick mayonnaise-like consistency. Stir in the lemon juice and correct the seasoning.

In a serving bowl combine the capsicum, onion, dressing and warm chickpeas. Sprinkle over the parsley and serve.

Plats principaux
Main dishes

Sole dieppoise
Poached sole with mussels and prawns in cider cream

Serves 4

The harbour town of Dieppe was influential in opening up the spice trade to Europe. As a consequence, the use of Asian spices is common throughout Normandy.

Traditionally, this dish was thickened with a roux, which I find a bit heavy and distracts from the fish. The reduction method intensifies the flavours and is enriched with cream. I like to use whole small prawns for a more intense prawn flavour, stunning presentation and a crunch. You could use fillets for this dish—you will need 8 fillets.

4 SMALL WHOLE SOLES OR FIRM FISH

2 SHALLOTS (ESCHALOTS), CHOPPED

250G (8OZ) CHAMPIGNONS

500G (17½OZ) MUSSELS

I LEEK, SLICED

¼ TEASPOON MILD CURRY POWDER

I BAY LEAF

250ML (8FL OZ/I CUP) DRY CIDER

30G (IOZ) BUTTER

125ML (4FL OZ/½ CUP) CREAM

250G (9OZ) SMALL PRAWNS, SHELLED AND DEVEINED

I TABLESPOON PARSLEY, CHOPPED

SALT AND PEPPER

Preheat the oven to 180°C (350°F). Trim the fins and spines off the fish with kitchen shears. Skin both sides and remove the roe. Butter an ovenproof dish and spread over the shallots and finely sliced mushrooms. Place the fish on top.

Steam the mussels with the leek, curry powder, bay leaf and cider. When the mussels have all opened, take off the heat; strain the cooking liquid and reserve. Shell the mussels and set aside. Pour the liquid over the sole, cover with buttered paper. and bake for about 12 minutes, until flesh comes away from the bones.

Transfer the fish and mushrooms to serving plates and keep warm. Strain the poaching liquid into a saucepan and reduce by two-thirds. Add the cream and reduce by half. Add the prawns to the sauce and poach gently for 2 minutes, then add the mussels and stir to warm through. Adjust the seasoning. Pour the sauce over the fish, scatter over the parsley and serve immediately.

Raie à la grenobloise
Skate wing with beurre noisette, capers, parsley and lemon

Serves 4

Skate may not be one of the premium fish on the market, but this perfectly follows the bistro economy and, with the rapid depletion of fishing stocks, use of the lesser fish makes sense. This dish can be made with other species but the skate flesh has a meaty, earthy flavour like no other fish. I often serve it with a scattering of deep-fried snails, which add texture and reinforce the earthy flavours.

1 TABLESPOON VEGETABLE OIL
100G (3½OZ) UNSALTED BUTTER
4 SKATE WINGS OR FIRM FISH
45G (1½OZ) LILLIPUT CAPERS
JUICE OF 1 LEMON
2 TABLESPOONS PARSLEY, CHOPPED

Heat a frying pan, then add the oil and 20g (⅔oz) of the butter. Add the skate and cook for 2 minutes on each side. Transfer the fish to serving plates. Add the remaining butter to the pan and increase the heat. As soon as the butter turns golden brown and gives off a nutty aroma, pour it over the fish. Deglaze the pan with the lemon juice, then add the capers and parsley. Toss the capers through to warm, then pour the butter over the fish and serve immediately.

Rouget à la Niçoise
Red mullet with fennel, tomato and orange salad

Serves 4

Red mullet is a delicate-flavoured fish and it has a similar texture and sweetness to crab. Purists say that they should be cooked whole—scales, guts and all. In France it is known as 'bécasse de mer', woodcock of the sea, because woodcock are also cooked ungutted.

Most of us are not fans of picking scales out of our teeth or being confronted with dozens of tiny fish bones—you can use fillets as well as whole fish.

8 RED MULLET, FILLETED, SKIN ON
   OR WHOLE FIRM FISH
I TABLESPOON OLIVE OIL
SALT AND PEPPER

SALAD
4 TOMATOES, PEELED AND SEEDED
I ORANGE, PEELED
2 BABY FENNEL BULBS

2 TABLESPOONS BLACK OLIVES,
   PITTED
4 ANCHOVY FILETS
I TABLESPOON CAPERS
2 TABLESPOONS OLIVE OIL
I TABLESPOON PARSLEY, COARSELY
   CHOPPED
JUICE OF I LEMON
SALT AND PEPPER

Cut the tomatoes into small dice. Cut the orange into segments. Wash and slice the fennel bulbs paper thin. Mix the tomatoes, oranges and fennel together with the remaining salad ingredients. Arrange on serving plates.

Preheat the grill. Place the mullet fillets, skin side up, on a buttered baking tray, season and drizzle with the olive oil. Cook under a hot grill until the skin crisps, about 1 minute; there is no need to turn them over. Top the salad with the fish and serve immediately.

Moules mariniére
Mussels in white wine

Serves 4

'Mariniére' is the simplest of the steamed mussel dishes. There are infinite variations on the basic recipe, but the most successful are the ones that don't mask the delicate flavour of the mussels. In Normandy, cider is used instead of wine and, curiously, adding a pinch of Indian curry powder is also common. A splash of cream will enrich and extend the flavour.

Excellent quality mussels are widely available 'pot ready'. I prefer the small blue ones. This dish requires no more than some crisp pommes frites and aïoli for dipping. You don't even need any cutlery. The 'correct' way to eat these is by using one of the mussel half shells as a makeshift spoon, scooping up the briny liquid as you go. Have a bowl for the empty shells and fingerbowls ready.

4KG (8LB 9OZ) MUSSELS
125G (4OZ) BUTTER
1 CLOVE GARLIC, CRUSHED
4 SHALLOTS (ESCHALOTS), SLICED
1 LEEK, SLICED
2 BAY LEAVES

½ BUNCH THYME, LEAVES STRIPPED
FROM THE STALKS
250ML (8FL OZ/1 CUP) WHITE WINE
PARSLEY TO GARNISH
PEPPER TO TASTE

Clean the mussels under running water, scrubbing off any dirt or seaweed and removing beards. In a large saucepan melt the butter and add the garlic, shallots, leek and herbs. Cook on a low heat until the vegetables are translucent. Add the mussels and the wine, cover, and turn up the heat to high. Cook, stirring occasionally until the mussels have just opened—this will take 3–5 minutes.

Discard any unopened mussels. Transfer to serving dishes and pour over the liquid. Garnish with the parsley. Season with pepper if you wish but never salt—the mussels will be salty enough.

Thon aux tomates rôties
Tuna steaks with roasted tomatoes

Serves 4

450G (1LB) ONIONS, SLICED

4 TABLESPOONS OLIVE OIL, PLUS A LITTLE EXTRA

500G (1LB 2OZ) SMALL TRUSS TOMATOES

4 CLOVES GARLIC, UNPEELED

1 TABLESPOON BALSAMIC VINEGAR

4 X 200G (7OZ) TUNA STEAKS

½ BUNCH THYME

2 BAY LEAVES

1 TABLESPOON PARSLEY, CHOPPED

SALT AND PEPPER

Preheat the oven to 200°C (400°F). Sauté the onions in 2 tablespoons of the olive oil until meltingly soft. Transfer to a gratin dish. Toss the tomatoes and garlic together with the remaining oil and balsamic. Add the tomatoes to the onions and roast in the heated oven for 20 minutes.

Rub the tuna steaks with olive oil. Sear the steaks in a very hot frying pan, then transfer to the gratin dish. Scatter over the thyme and bay leaves and bake for 10 minutes. Season, sprinkle over the parsley and serve.

Morue en bouillabaisse
Bouillabaisse of salt cod

Serves 4

Bouillabaisse calls for a vast array of small rockfish and crustaceans. In southern France this mix of fish is widely available pot-ready in markets and simply sold as 'bouillabaisse'. This is a simplified version using salt cod.

Due to its proximity to North Africa, Moroccan spices have become commonplace in Marseille. I like to add ras el hanout, which literally means 'top of the shop'.

900G (2LB) SALT COD OR FIRM
   SALTED FISH
PINCH OF SAFFRON
250ML (8FL OZ/1 CUP) WHITE WINE
4 TABLESPOONS OLIVE OIL
2 ONIONS, SLICED
1 LEEK, SLICED
1 FENNEL BULB, SLICED

4 CLOVES GARLIC
1 TEASPOON RAS EL HANOUT
3.5CM (1½-IN) STRIP ORANGE PEEL
BOUQUET GARNI
50G (12OZ) TOMATOES, SKINNED
   AND DESEEDED
500ML (16FL OZ/2 CUPS) FISH
   STOCK OR WATER

Soak the salt cod in cold water for 24 hours, changing the water at least every 8 hours. Once desalted, remove skin and bones and cut into 4 pieces.

Sprinkle the saffron over the wine and set aside.

Heat the olive oil in a casserole and gently cook the onions, leek, fennel and garlic without colouring. Add the ras el hanout and continue to cook until fragrant. Pour in the infused wine, orange peel, bouquet garni and tomatoes. Cook, stirring frequently, until the tomatoes have collapsed, then add the fish stock or water.

Add the fish to the casserole and poach on a low heat with the lid on for 5–10 minutes, depending on the thickness. Discard the bouquet garni and serve.

Serve with potatoes cooked with saffron and a dish of rouille (see page 13) with croutons.

La bourride
Garlic fish stew

Serves 4

This lesser known cousin of bouillabaisse is based on the same principle, but this is a white stew thickened with aïoli rather than tomatoes and rouille. Use firm-fleshed fish such as John Dory, whiting or gurnard. Serve the bourride with toasts or boiled potatoes.

1 TABLESPOON OLIVE OIL

1 ONION, SLICED

1 LEEK, SLICED

2 BABY FENNEL BULBS, QUARTERED

1 LITRE (36FL OZ/4 CUPS) FISH
STOCK

2 BAY LEAVES

4 SPRIGS OF THYME

¼ TEASPOON GROUND ALLSPICE

1 KG (2LB 4OZ) FISH FILLETS OR
WHOLE SMALL FISH

250G (9OZ) BABY SQUID, CLEANED

150ML (5FL OZ/⅔ CUP) AÏOLI (SEE
RECIPE, PAGE 13)

2 EGG YOLKS

SALT AND PEPPER

Heat the oil in a casserole and sweat off the onion, leek and fennel until translucent. Add the stock, bay leaves, thyme and allspice. Cook uncovered on a low heat for 10 minutes. Add the fish to the pot and poach for 5 minutes, then add the squid and cook for a further minute. Remove the casserole from the heat.

Using a slotted spoon, transfer the fish, squid and vegetables to individual serving plates.

Whisk together the aïoli and egg yolks in a soup tureen, then gradually incorporate the hot stock, a spoonful at a time. Adjust the seasoning and pour over the fish.

Saumon au beurre blanc
Poached salmon with butter sauce

Serves 4

Poaching in a court bouillon is a failsafe way of retaining the delicate flavour and moisture in fish. I often stir a few shredded sorrel leaves through the sauce just before serving.

4 x 200G (7OZ) SALMON FILLETS
I TABLESPOON SALMON ROE

COURT BOUILLON
125ML (4FL OZ/½ CUP) WHITE WINE
500ML (9FL OZ/2 CUPS) WATER
I LEEK, SLICED
I CARROT, SLICED
BOUQUET GARNI
½ LEMON

BEURRÉ BLANC
3 TABLESPOONS WHITE WINE
3 TABLESPOONS WHITE WINE
   VINEGAR
2 SHALLOTS (ESCHALOTS), CHOPPED
I SPRIG OF THYME
225G (8OZ) BUTTER, COLD, CUT INTO
   2.5-CM (I-IN) CUBES
SALT AND PEPPER

To make the court bouillon, combine all the ingredients in a saucepan and bring to a simmer. Cook uncovered for 10 minutes, then add the salmon and turn off the heat. Leave to sit for 10 minutes.

For the beurre blanc, combine the wine, vinegar, shallots and thyme in a saucepan. Bring to the boil and reduce to 1 tablespoon. Remove the pan from the heat and whisk in the butter a cube at a time, ensuring that it is fully incorporated before each addition. Pass the sauce through a fine sieve, then add the sorrel and season.

Remove the salmon from the bouillon. Place on warmed serving plates. Spoon over the sauce and some roe. Serve immediately.

Steak frites
Steak and chips

Serves 4

Steak and chips is a quintessentially French dish. Every bistro has its own version, be it sirloin or entrecôte, a humble onglet or the king of steaks, the côte de boeuf. Whatever the cut you choose, always buy the best quality you can afford. Beef that has been correctly fed and aged will be the most rewarding.

4 X 250G (9OZ) STEAKS, YOUR CHOICE OF CUT
4 TABLESPOONS VEGETABLE OIL
SALT AND PEPPER
QUANTITY OF POMMES FRITE (SEE PAGE 152)

Have the steaks ready at room temperature. Coat with the oil and season well. Place on a medium hot grill or barbecue. Cook for 2–3 minutes, then turn and cook for a further 3 minutes for a rare steak or 5–6 minutes for medium. Leave to rest for a few minutes.

You may top the steak with a slice of beurre café de Paris (see next recipe) or another flavoured butter.

Beurre cafè de Paris
Parisienne butter

250G (9OZ) UNSALTED BUTTER, AT ROOM TEMPERATURE
2 CLOVES GARLIC, CRUSHED
I ANCHOVY FILLET, FINELY CHOPPED
I TEASPOON CAPERS, FINELY CHOPPED
I TEASPOON CORNICHONS, FINELY CHOPPED
2 TABLESPOONS PARSLEY, FINELY CHOPPED
2 SHALLOTS (ESCHALOTS), FINELY CHOPPED

1 TABLESPOON COGNAC

1 TABLESPOON MADEIRA

¼ TEASPOON MILD CURRY POWDER

PEPPER

Soften the butter, then add the remaining ingredients and mix throughly. Form into a log shape using plastic film, twisting and tying each end to seal. Store in the refrigerator. Slice off pieces as needed.

Bavette aux échalotes
Flank steak with caramelised shallots

Serves 4

What the flank cut lacks in tenderness, it makes up for in a big way on flavour. Bistros are synonymous with efficient use of lesser grade cuts and the bavette is the steak of choice for many.

60G (2OZ) BUTTER

20 SHALLOTS (ESCHALOTS), SLICED

1 SPRIG THYME, CHOPPED

1 BAY LEAF

2 TABLESPOONS RED WINE VINEGAR

4 X 250G (9OZ) FLANK STEAKS

2 TABLESPOONS VEGETABLE OIL

1 CLOVE GARLIC, CRUSHED

2 TABLESPOONS PORT

250ML (8FL OZ/1 CUP) RED WINE

500ML (2 CUPS) BEEF STOCK

1 TABLESPOON PARSLEY, FINELY
  CHOPPED

SALT AND PEPPER

In a casserole, melt the butter and add the shallots, thyme and bay leaf. Sauté over a medium heat until golden brown, then deglaze with the vinegar and season. Keep warm.

Trim the steaks of any excess sinew. Season well. Heat the oil in a heavy-based frying pan, and cook the steaks on a high heat for 3 minutes each side. Remove the steaks to rest. Add the garlic to the pan and sauté until lightly coloured. Add the port and wine and reduce to a glaze. Pour in the stock and reduce further to a sauce consistency. Adjust seasoning.

Top the steaks with the caramelised shallots, pour over the sauce and garnish with parsley.

Serve with steamed green beans, frites or salad.

Boeuf bourguignon
Braised beef in red wine

Serves 4

Perhaps the most famous and loved of all the bistro staples, originally boeuf bourguignon was made with one piece of beef larded with bacon fat to keep the meat moist. Nowadays it is more common to cut the beef into large dice. The bacon still remains, not for larding, but just because of its bacon flavour.

It's essential to use a cut of beef with a high content of connective tissue—rump or chuck are ideal choices. I often use less traditional cuts like brisket and cheek, although my personal favourites are oxtail and short ribs (the flavour of beef cooked on the bone is unsurpassed).

4 TABLESPOONS VEGETABLE OIL
1KG (2LB 4OZ) BEEF RUMP, CUT INTO
   5-CM (2-IN) DICE
30G (1OZ) FLOUR
1 ONION, QUARTERED
1 CARROT, LARGE SLICE
4 CLOVES GARLIC
750ML (24FLOZ/3 CUPS) RED WINE,
   PREFERABLY BURGUNDY

500ML (16FL OZ/2 CUPS) BEEF
   STOCK
1 BOUQUET GARNI
30G (1OZ) BUTTER
16 BABY ONIONS
200G (7OZ) THICK FATTY BACON,
   CUT INTO LARDONS
250G (9OZ) CHAMPIGNONS,
   QUARTERED
PARSLEY, FINELY CHOPPED, TO
   GARNISH

Preheat the oven to 150°C (300°F). Heat the oil in a heavy-bottomed casserole. Toss the beef in flour. Brown the beef in the oil—in small batches, so the pan is not overcrowded—and remove. In the same pan sautè the onion, carrot and garlic until browned. Return the beef to the pan and add wine, stock and bouquet garni. Bring to a gentle simmer and then place the casserole in the oven for 3–4 hours.

Once the beef is tender (but not falling apart), remove from the sauce with a slotted spoon; set aside and keep warm. Strain the sauce into a clean pan and reduce if necessary. Adjust the seasoning.

For the garnish, gently heat the butter in a sautè pan on a low heat and cook the baby onions until tender and glazed; add the onions to the beef. In the same pan, fry off the lardons and mushrooms until golden brown (add more butter in necessary). Pour off any excess fat and add to the beef.

Return the beef to the cleaned casserole, pour over the sauce and stir through the lardons and mushrooms. Bring back to a simmer. Serve the beef sprinkled with chopped parsley and a dish of boiled potatoes or pommes purée (see page 154).

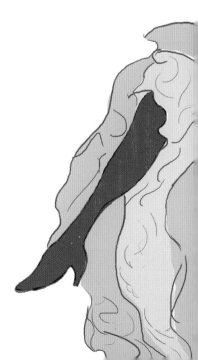

Oiseaux sans tête
Beef braised in beer

Serves 4

Oiseaux sans tête literally translates as 'birds without heads'. I'm not sure why—it bears little resemblance to anything avian. Whatever, it is a great dish. Think of it as a complex sausage with onion gravy.

For best results use a Belgium beer such as Chimay or Leffe or a stout. Drink the same beer with the paupiettes and accompany them with boiled or mashed potatoes.

4 X 150G (5OZ) TOPSIDE OR RUMP STEAKS

350G (12OZ) MINCED BEEF OR PORK

1 EGG

2 SHALLOTS (ESCHALOTS), CHOPPED

30G (1OZ) FRESH BREADCRUMBS

LEAVES FROM 1 STALK OF ROSEMARY, CHOPPED

1 TABLESPOON PARSLEY, CHOPPED

1 TABLESPOON FLOUR

45G (1½OZ) BUTTER

1 ONION, SLICED

750ML (24FLOZ/3 CUPS) BEER

185ML (6FL OZ/¾ CUP) BEEF STOCK

2 BAY LEAVES

SALT AND PEPPER

BUTCHERS' TWINE

Preheat the oven to 160°C (325°F). Place the steaks between plastic film and beat to 3mm (¼in) thickness.

Prepare the stuffing by combining the minced meat, egg, shallots, breadcrumbs, rosemary and parsley. Mix thoroughly and season well. Divide the mix into four, place in the centre of each steak and roll up into a rough sausage shape. Secure the paupiettes with butchers' twine and dust with the flour. Melt the butter in a casserole and brown the paupiettes on all sides. Remove and set aside.

Add the onions to the casserole and cook until caramelised. Pour in the beer, and stock, add the bay leaves and reduce by half. Return the paupiettes to the casserole and cook in a oven with the lid on for 45 minutes.

Transfer the paupiettes to serving plates. Remove the strings. Reduce the sauce if necessary and adjust the seasoning. Pour over the sauce and serve.

Gras-double lyonnaise
Beef tripe with caramelised onions and tomatoes

Serves 4

You may have preconceptions about tripe. I urge you to a least give it a try. Bouchons, the Lyon equivalent of bistros, are famous for their tripe dishes, particularly the tripe sausage andouillette. Tripe has little flavour on its own—it is prized for its textural qualities and its ability to absorb flavours. Gras-double is the term for smooth flat tripe, but the honeycomb variety is fine to use also.

1KG (2LB 4OZ) TRIPE
1 OIGNON CLOUTE (SEE PAGE 236)
6 TABLESPOONS VEGETABLE OIL
4 ONIONS, SLICED
8 CLOVES GARLIC, CRUSHED
2 TABLESPOONS RED WINE VINEGAR

125ML (4FL OZ/½ CUP) RED WINE
250ML (8FL OZ/1 CUP) BEEF STOCK
450G (1LB) TOMATOES, SKINNED,
    DESEEDED AND CHOPPED
SALT AND PEPPER

Place the tripe in a large saucepan, cover with cold water and bring to the boil. Drain off the hot water and top up with cold water again. Add the oignon cloute and bring to the boil again. Simmer covered for 3 hours. Pour off the water, discard the oignon cloute and leave to cool in a colander. Once cooled, cut into 5-cm (2-in) thick strips.

In a casserole heat a little of the oil and cook the onions until golden brown. Remove the onion from the casserole and set aside. In the remaining oil, sauté the tripe pieces until well coloured and crisp. Return the caramelised onion to the casserole with the remaining ingredients. Cover and simmer for 1 hour.

Discard the bouquet garni and adjust the seasoning. Serve hot.

Pot-au-feu

Serves 4

This dish is the ultimate 'one-pot wonder'—a selection of meltingly tender meats, aromatic vegetables and buttery marrow bones, all gently poached together until their flavours permeate a rich broth. It has its roots in mediaeval times, when food was cooked in a cauldron over an open fire. Hence its translation: 'pot of fire'.

To obtain a clear broth—the hallmark of a good pot au feu—the liquid must never boil. It should be kept at scarcely a simmer. The dish may be presented as two courses, the broth served first with the marrow scooped out onto toasts, and the meat and vegetables served as a main course with condiments. I prefer to serve it as one dish. Serving the broth together with the meat avoids the risk of the meat becoming dry. Accompany the pot au feu with baguettes on which to spread the marrow, Dijon mustard, cornichons and coarse salt.

500G (17½OZ) BEEF BRISKET

500G (17½OZ) BEEF SHORT RIBS

500G (17½OZ) OXTAIL, CUT INTO
  5CM (2IN) LENGTHS

3 CLOVES GARLIC

1 ONION, HALVED

2 CLOVES

4 CARROTS, CUT INTO DISKS

4 LEEKS, WHITE ONLY, CUT
  LENGTHWAYS

2 TURNIPS, CUT IN HALF

2 POTATOES, HALVED

1 BOUQUET GARNI

5 PEPPERCORNS

1 CINNAMON STICK

4 MARROW BONES, CUT INTO
  5-CM (2-IN) LENGTHS

PARSLEY, FINELY CHOPPED, TO
  GARNISH

SALT AND PEPPER

Place the meats in a large stockpot. Cover with cold water and bring to the boil. Skim off all the impurities. Lower the heat to a very gentle simmer and continue to cook for 2 hours, skimming frequently.

Stud one onion half with the cloves. Brown the cut surface of the other half in a hot, dry frying pan. Add the studded onion, the other vegetables, the bouquet garni, peppercorns and cinnamon to the stockpot. Cook for a further 1½ hours.

CONTINUES ON PAGE 118

Wrap the marrow bones in muslin. Add to the stock pot and cook for another 20 minutes.

Discard the bouquet garni, onion and cinnamon. Transfer the meats to a cutting board and the vegetables and marrow bones to a platter. Keep warm.

Skim off all the fat from the broth. Bring to the boil and reduce by half until you have a concentrated, well-flavoured broth. Season to taste.

Carve the meats into serving portions. Unwrap the marrow bones. Distribute pieces of the meats, a marrow bone and vegetables into deep bowls. Pour over the broth and sprinkle with parsley.

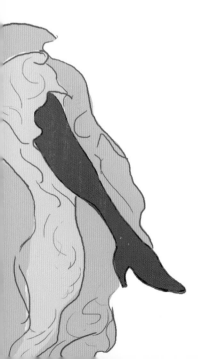

Steak tartare
Raw ground beef steak

Serves 4

Steak tartare is a very personal thing. There are as many variations as there are chefs. Some like to use premium cuts like fillet, but I don't think it's tasty enough and is a waste of a beautiful cut. Some use highly marbled beef like wagyu, but I say it's too rich and doesn't have a nice mouth feel. Some say you must cut the steak by hand, but I prefer using a mincing machine, which gives a better consistency. Find what works for you, but never use store-brought minced beef.

If eating tartare as a main meal sounds overwhelming, reduce the quantities and serve as a starter with toast.

750 G (1LB 10OZ) BEEF SIRLOIN OR SCOTCH

20ML (⅔FL OZ) OLIVE OIL

4 EGG YOLKS

2 TABLESPOONS CAPERS, CHOPPED

2 TABLESPOONS CORNICHONS, CHOPPED

4 SHALLOTS (ESCHALOTS), CHOPPED

2 TABLESPOONS PARSLEY, CHOPPED

SALT AND PEPPER

TABASCO SAUCE

WORCESTERSHIRE SAUCE

Remove all sinew and excess fat from the beef. Cut finely by hand or use a mincer if you prefer. Moisten the beef with the olive oil and season. Mix well.

Mould into dome shapes and flatten the tops; make an indent in the centres and pour a yolk into each. Place on 4 serving plates and arrange small mounds of the capers, cornichons, shallots and parsley around the beef. Alternatively, the garnish can be mixed into the beef before serving. I prefer the former method, as it allows your guests to add what they wish.

Serve immediately with your choice of a crisp green salad or pommes frites (page 152) and aïoli, and the sauces on the side.

Foie de veau pôelé, jus à l'aigre-doux

Pan-fried veal liver with sweet and sour sauce

Serves 4

'Aigre' translates as sour and 'doux' as sweet. Don't be put off by memories of cloying Chinese sweet and sour sauce. This preparation is a delicate blend of sweet port and a fruity vinegar.

If liver is not to your liking, this sauce works equally well with other rich meats, particularly duck magret. I like to serve it on a mound of garlicky iron-rich spinach to complement the liver, and with pommes frite of course.

2 TABLESPOONS BUTTER OR DUCK FAT, PLUS 1 TABLESPOON BUTTER

4 SLICES VEAL LIVER, 2CM (¾IN) THICK

2 SHALLOTS (ESCHALOTS), CHOPPED

1 CLOVE GARLIC, CRUSHED

2 TABLESPOONS RASPBERRY VINEGAR

3 TABLESPOONS PORT

250ML (8FL OZ/1 CUP) BEEF STOCK

SALT AND PEPPER

Heat the 2 tablespoons of butter or fat in a heavy-based frying pan. Season the liver and put it in the pan; sauté on high heat for 2 minutes on each side until crisped and brown. Don't overcook the liver—it should have some give when touched. Transfer the liver to serving plates and keep warm.

Pour off the excess cooking fat and add the shallots and garlic to the pan. Cook until slightly coloured. Add the vinegar and deglaze the pan, stirring in the reduced meat juices. Pour in the port and reduce to a syrupy glaze. Add the stock and reduce by half. Take the pan off the heat, whisk in 1 tablespoon of butter to thicken the sauce and give it a glossy sheen. Adjust the seasoning. Pour the sauce over the liver and serve.

Blanquette de veau
Veal breast stew

Serves 4

Veal breast is a highly underrated cut. It has good proportions of fat, lean meat and connective tissues, making it ideal for slow cooking. The bones should be included in the cooking pot. The calf's breast bones are cartilaginous rather than fully developed. This cartilage, and the connective tissues, renders down during the cooking to enrich the dish.

1KG (2LB 4OZ) VEAL BREAST ON THE BONE, IN 5-CM (2-IN) DICE

2 CARROTS, QUARTERED LENGTHWAYS

2 CELERY STALKS

1 OIGNON CLOUTE (SEE PAGE 236)

1 BOUQUET GARNI

500ML (16FL OZ/2 CUPS) CHICKEN STOCK

60G (2OZ) BUTTER

30G (1OZ) FLOUR

20 PEARL ONIONS, PEELED

200G (7OZ) CHAMPIGNONS, QUARTERED

125ML (4FL OZ/½ CUP) CREAM

2 EGG YOLKS

SALT AND WHITE PEPPER

Add veal to a large pan of boiling salted water, bring back to boil and cook for 5 minutes, skimming to remove impurities. Strain in a colander; discard liquid.

Prepare a bouillon by combining the carrot, celery, oignon cloute and bouquet garni in a casserole with the chicken stock. Add the blanched veal. Bring to a gentle simmer, cover, and cook on low heat for about 1½ hours, until the veal is tender but not falling apart. Carefully remove the veal pieces and set aside.

Strain cooking liquid through a fine sieve; discard the vegetables and aromatics. You should have about 600ml (19fl oz) of liquid; if not, top up with more chicken stock. Melt the butter in cleaned casserole. Add in the flour and cook gently without colouring for 2 minutes. Pour in cooking liquid in small batches, stirring vigorously to discourage lumps. Once all the liquid has been added, return the veal along with the pearl onions and mushrooms. Cover and cook gently for 15 minutes. Mix the cream and egg yolks; remove from the heat and stir into the casserole (to thicken and add sheen to the stew). Adjust seasoning. Serve with a pilaf.

Côtelettes de veau Vallee d'Auge
Veal in cider and calvados sauce with apples

Serves 4

This recipe comes from the apple-producing region of the Auge River in Normandy. When you see a dish from Normandy it almost always has apples, calvados or cream as standard ingredients. This lucky one has all three.

45G (1½OZ) BUTTER, PLUS 30G (1OZ)

4 X 200G (7OZ) VEAL CHOPS

20 PEARL ONIONS, PEELED

2 GRANNY SMITH APPLES, PEELED AND CORED

3 TABLESPOONS CALVADOS

185 ML (6FL OZ/¾ CUP) DRY CIDER

125G (4OZ) CRÈME FRAÎCHE

SALT AND PEPPER

Heat 45g butter in a large frying pan and sauté the chops until well browned and cooked to the desired doneness. While the chops are cooking, simmer the onions in salted water until tender. Cut each apple into 8 pieces and, in a separate pan, fry them in the 30g butter until they are golden and cooked but still retain a slight crunch.

When the chops are done, remove them from the pan and add in the onions. Cook briefly to colour, then put back the chops. Pour in the calvados and flambé by lighting; stand back and wait until the flames have subsided. Then add the cider and reduce to a light syrup. Take the pan from the heat and stir through the crème fraîche and adjust the seasoning. Serve garnished with the apples.

Navarin printanier
Lamb with spring vegetables

Serves 4

This casserole announces the arrival of spring: it incorporates the new season's lamb and the glorious young vegetables—especially sweet turnips, because you can't have a navarin without navets. You can substitute frozen peas for fresh and use good-quality bottled artichoke hearts. But I urge you to use fresh—this is a celebration of spring's bounty after all. Serve the dish with a pilaf or buttered new potatoes.

1KG (2LB 4OZ) LEG OF LAMB OR
   SHOULDER, DEBONED

3 TABLESPOONS OLIVE OIL

1 ONION, CHOPPED

1 CLOVE GARLIC, CRUSHED

200ML (7FL OZ) CHICKEN STOCK

2 TOMATOES, PEELED AND CHOPPED

1 BOUQUET GARNI

4 GLOBE ARTICHOKE HEARTS 1
   BUNCH BABY TURNIPS, TRIMMED

1 BUNCH DUTCH CARROTS, TRIMMED

1 BUNCH ASPARAGUS, TRIMMED

150G (5OZ) SHELLED FRESH PEAS

1 TABLESPOON PARSLEY, CHOPPED

SALT AND PEPPER

Cut the lamb into large cubes. Heat the oil in a casserole and brown the meat—you will have to do this in batches. Set the meat aside. Add the onion and garlic to the casserole and cook until translucent. Put the lamb back in the casserole along with the stock, tomatoes and bouquet garni. Place on the lid and on a low heat simmer for 1 hour.

Add the artichoke hearts, turnips and carrots to the casserole and cook for a further 45 minutes. Blanch the asparagus and peas together for about a minute in boiling salted water. Discard the bouquet garni.

Remove the lamb and vegetables from the casserole with a slotted spoon and transfer to serving plates. Skim off the excess fat from the sauce in the casserole and reduce the liquid if necessary. Scatter the blanched asparagus and peas over the meat, pour over the sauce and garnish with chopped parsley.

Gigot d'agneau aux flageolets
Roast leg of lamb with flageolet beans

Serves 4

Rich creamy flageolets have an affinity with lamb, although white haricot or red kidney also work well. Salt marsh lamb is undoubtedly the best but also try mutton, which has a more pronounced flavour.

2 KG (4LB 6OZ) LAMB LEG, BONE IN
2 CLOVES GARLIC, CUT INTO SLIVERS
½ BUNCH THYME
2 TABLESPOONS OLIVE OIL
4 SLICES WHITE BREAD
6 TABLESPOONS PARSLEY, CHOPPED
1 TABLESPOON DIJON MUSTARD
125ML (4FL OZ/½ CUP) WHITE WINE
SALT AND PEPPER

FOR THE BEANS
350G (12OZ) DRIED FLAGEOLET
  BEANS
1 ONION, CHOPPED
2 CLOVES GARLIC
1 CELERY STICK, DICED
1 CARROT, DICED
1 BOUQUET GARNI

Soak beans overnight, drain and rinse. Sauté the onion, garlic, celery and carrot until soft but not coloured. Add the beans and bouquet garni. Cover with water and simmer uncovered for about 1½ hours, until tender. You may need to top up the water during cooking. Discard the bouquet garni.

Preheat the oven to 200°C (400°F). Cut small incisions in the lamb flesh, insert small slivers of garlic and thyme. Rub the leg with salt and pepper and drizzle over the oil. Roast in a roasting dish for 40 minutes.

Combine the bread and parsley in a food processor and blend until you have a fine green crumb. Spread the mustard over the lamb and then coat with the crumb mix. Return the meat to the oven for 10–15 minutes until crisp.

Transfer the lamb to a cutting board to rest for 15 minutes before carving. Pour off any excess fat from the roasting dish, add the wine and return to the heat, stirring in the reduced meat juices from the pan, then add the cooked beans. Adjust the seasoning and serve the beans with the sliced lamb.

Petit salé aux lentilles
Salt pork with lentils du Puy

Serves 4

Petit sale literally means 'lightly salted'. It's a charcuterie staple and is used in a variety of dishes such as cassoulet, choucroute and potee. Earthy lentils are the perfect foil for the petit sale's rich brininess. Or try it with fresh green peas, dried beans, cabbage or potato salad. The pork will need to brined for at least two days.

1KG (2LB 4OZ) PORK BELLY

BRINE
500G (17½OZ) ROCK SALT
75G (2½OZ) SUGAR
1 TABLESPOON SALTPETRE
4 BAY LEAVES
1 TABLESPOON BLACK PEPPERCORNS
4 CLOVES

LENTILS
250G (9OZ) LENTILS DU PUY
2 CLOVES GARLIC, CRUSHED
1 CARROT, DICED
1 CELERY STICK, DICED
1 OIGNON CLOUTE (SEE PAGE 236)
1 BOUQUET GARNI

Combining all the brine ingredients with 2.5 litres (64fl oz/8 cups) of water. Bring to the boil and simmer for 15 minutes, then strain through a sieve and cool completely. Place the pork in a non-corrosive container and cover with the brine. Cover and refrigerate for at least 2 days, up to 1 week.

Pour off the brine and refill the container with water, then soak for 1 hour. Put the pork in a large saucepan and cover with fresh water. Bring to the boil and simmer for 10 minutes. Taste the water—if it's too salty, start over with fresh water. Continue cooking at a gentle simmer for 45 minutes, then add the lentils, vegetables and herbs. Cook for a further 1 hour, until the lentils are tender.

Côte de porc charcutiere
Grilled pork with mustard and cornichon sauce

Serves 4

This is bistro fare at its finest. Simple ingredients, minimum fuss, big flavour.
It is so named because it was readily available at the pork butcher's, la charcutier.

2 TABLESPOONS VEGETABLE OIL

4 X 250G (9OZ) PORK LOIN CHOPS

4 SHALLOTS (ESCHALOTS), CHOPPED

2 TABLESPOONS CIDER VINEGAR

200ML (7FL OZ/¾ CUP) WHITE WINE

250ML (8FL OZ/1 CUP) BEEF STOCK

2 TOMATOES, PEELED, DESEEDED AND CHOPPED

½ TABLESPOON DIJON MUSTARD

2 TABLESPOONS CORNICHONS, CUT INTO MATCHSTICKS

SALT AND PEPPER

Heat the oil in a large heavy-based frying pan. Season the chops and sautè on a medium heat until cooked through and golden brown on both sides. Transfer to serving plates and keep warm.

Pour off all but 2 tablespoons of the fat from the pan. Add the shallots and cook until golden. Pour in the vinegar to deglaze the pan, stirring to incorporate the reduced meat juices. Add in the wine and reduce by half. Then add the stock and tomatoes and reduce by half again. Stir in the mustard and the cornichons. Adjust the seasoning. Spoon the sauce over the chops and serve.

Le cassoulet de Castelnaudary
Slow braise of sausage, duck and white beans

Serves 4

This humble peasant dish from the southwest of France has been elevated to one of the great dishes of French cooking. Most towns of the region have their own variation, and needless to say there is great debate about which is best. Ingredients range from mutton, smoked sausage, calves' feet and pork rinds. The one thing that always remains the same are the beans, which are the star of the dish—the rest is just garnish. The name 'cassoulet' comes from the cassole d'issel, an earthenware cooking vessel from the town of Issel, near Castelnaudary. The original version calls for confit of goose, which can be difficult to obtain, so I have replaced it with confit of duck. Make your own confit or excellent canned ones are available from France.

500G (17½OZ) DRIED WHITE
  HARICOT BEANS
1 ONION, CHOPPED
150G (5OZ) PETIT SALÉ OR BACON
4 CLOVES GARLIC, CRUSHED, PLUS
  ½ CLOVE FOR RUBBING
625ML (20FL OZ/2½ CUP) CHICKEN
  STOCK
2 TOMATOES, PEELED, DESEEDED
  AND CHOPPED

1 BOUQUET GARNI
1 SMALL OIGNON CLOUTE (SEE
  PAGE 236)
2 CONFIT DUCK LEGS
4 TOULOUSE SAUSAGES (COARSE
  GARLIC PORK)
60G (2OZ) BREADCRUMBS
2 TABLESPOONS CHOPPED PARSLEY

Soak the beans overnight. The next day, drain the beans, put them in a saucepan and cover with water. Cook gently for about 2 hours, until the beans are partially cooked. Drain.

In the meantime prepare the cooking liquid by sautéing the onion, petit salé and crushed garlic in a little of the fat from the duck. Once slightly browned, add the stock, tomatoes, bouquet garni and oignon cloute. Bring to the boil and simmer for 30 minutes, then discard the bouquet garni and the oignon cloute.

Preheat the oven to 150°C (300°F). Rub the inside of the cassoulet dish with half a clove of garlic. Place the confit, the sausages and petit salé taken from the stock in the dish. Then add the drained beans. Top with the liquid and bring to the boil. Sprinkle the breadcrumbs mixed with the parsley over the beans. Place in the heated oven for about 1 hour until the beans are meltingly soft and a crisp crust has formed.

Confit de cuisse de canard
Crisp-fried preserved duck

Serves 4

Confit is a method of preserving. The meat is salted then cooked and packed in its own fat. Canned or fresh duck fat is available at most good supermarkets.

Serve the duck with bitter greens and walnut and some potatoes fried in the same fat or with carrot cumin puree and caramelised witlof.

You will need to commence preparation the day before.

4 X 220G (7½OZ) DUCK MARYLANDS, SKIN ON, BONE IN
600ML (21FL OZ/2½ CUP) DUCK FAT

MARINADE
30G (1OZ) ROCK SALT
2 TEASPOONS CRACKED BLACK PEPPER

½ BUNCH PARSLEY
2 SHALLOTS (ESCHALOTS)
1 CLOVE GARLIC
¼ BUNCH THYME
1 BAY LEAF

Combine all the marinade ingredients in a food processor and blend until coarsely chopped. Rub the duck with the marinade. Cover and refrigerate over night.

The following day, preheat the oven to 150°C (300°F). Rinse the duck thoroughly and pat dry. Place duck in a casserole and cover with the fat. Cover and cook in a oven for about 2 hours, until the flesh is very tender but not falling off the bone. Cool the duck in the fat and refrigerate until needed.

To serve, slightly heat the casserole to release the duck from the fat (which will have set hard). Shallow-fry the duck, skin side down, in a heavy-based frying pan. Slow careful cooking will yield a crisp result—this may take about 10 minutes. Once the skin is crisp, turn and cook for a further 2 minutes. Drain on paper towels and serve.

Magret de canard aux pêches
Duck breast with peaches

Serves 4

A true magret is the breast of ducks reared for foie gras production. The term is now commonly applied to all farmed duck. The magret is texturally similar to beef steak and, like steak, is best cooked to medium rare. Fruit is an excellent counterbalance to this rich meat, and figs and cherries work just as well as peaches.

4 PEACHES, STONED AND HALVED

185ML (6FL OZ/¾ CUP) VERJUS

1 TABLESPOON THYME, CHOPPED

1 BAY LEAF

4 X 200G (7OZ) DUCK BREASTS

1 TEASPOON QUATRE ÉPICES

2 SHALLOTS (ESCHALOTS), CHOPPED

2 TABLESPOONS ARMANGNAC

250ML (8FL OZ/1 CUP) BEEF STOCK

SALT AND PEPPER

Preheat the oven to 200°C (400°F). Cut the peaches in half, remove the stones. Place the peach halves in a casserole, cut sides down, pour over the verjus and add the thyme and bay leaf. Cover and bake in the heated oven for 35 minutes. Let cool and remove the peach skins, pass through a sieve and reserve the cooking liquid.

Trim any sinew off the breasts and score the skin in a criss-cross pattern. Dust the breasts with the quatre épices and season. Heat a heavy skillet or frying pan until hot. Add the breasts, skin side down—enough fat will be rendered from the duck, so no other fat is needed. Cook for 2 minutes until the skin is crisp, turn and cook for a further 5 minutes. Keep the duck in a warm place to rest.

Discard the fat, except 1 tablespoon, from the pan. Add the shallots and sauté until golden, then add the armagnac and flambé by lighting; stand back and wait until the flames have subsided. Pour in the reserved peach cooking liquid. Bring to the boil and reduce to a syrup. Add the stock and peaches. Reduce the sauce to a thick consistency. Taste and season.

Cut the duck into thick slices and arrange with the peaches on serving plates. Pour over the sauce.

Coq au vin
Chicken braised in red wine

Serves 4

Originally this was a recipe intended for use with old cockerels that were too tough and unsuitable for roasting. The use of a standard chicken does reduce cooking times, but unfortunately there's also a loss in the characteristic flavour. Be sure to use a good-quality wine, which will make all the difference, plus you want to enjoy a glass yourself while you're cooking.

1 X 1.6KG (3LB 8OZ) CHICKEN

100G (3½OZ) THICK FATTY BACON, CUT INTO LARDONS

30G (1OZ) BUTTER

16 SMALL PEARL ONIONS

200G (7OZ) BUTTON MUSHROOMS QUARTERED

1 TABLESPOON FLOUR

500ML (16FL OZ/2 CUPS) RED WINE

2 CLOVES GARLIC CRUSHED

1 BOUQUET GARNI

1 TABLESPOON PARSLEY, CHOPPED

SALT AND PEPPER

Cut the chicken into eight pieces. Heat a heavy-bottomed casserole, add the lardons and gently fry in the butter until the fat is released and lightly golden. Remove the lardons and keep to one side. Repeat the browning process with the chicken, cooking it first on the skin side and then turning it. Brown the onions next, and finally the mushrooms.

Discard all but 2 tablespoons of the fat, sprinkle in the flour and cook gently until lightly browned. Stir in the red wine and return the chicken, lardons, pearl onions and mushrooms to the casserole with the garlic and bouquet garni. Simmer on a low heat or in a preheated 175°C (350°C) oven for 30–40 minutes. Taste for seasoning.

Serve in the casserole sprinkled with chopped parsley. Accompany with pommes puree or steamed green beans.

Poulet aux quarante gousses d'ail
Pot-roasted chicken with 40 cloves of garlic

Serves 4

Don't be put off by the overwhelming quantity of garlic. After pot-roasting the garlic mellows to a nutty creaminess. This dish will only be as good as the chicken you choose. Use certified organic—you will notice the difference.

1 X 1.5KG (3LB 5OZ) CHICKEN
1 BOUQUET GARNI
40 CLOVES GARLIC, UNPEELED
250ML (8FL OZ/1 CUP) WHITE WINE
4 TABLESPOONS OLIVE OIL
SALT AND PEPPER
BAGUETTE TO SERVE

Preheat the oven to 180°C (350°F). Pat the chicken dry, season generously with salt and pepper and insert the bouquet garni into its cavity. Prepare the garlic by breaking up the bulbs and removing all the excess papery skin, but don't peel. Put the garlic cloves and wine into a casserole and place the chicken, breast side up, on top. Drizzle with the oil. Line the rim of the casserole with aluminum foil and cover with the lid to form a tight seal. Bake in the oven for 1½ hours.

Let the chicken rest for 10 minutes. Carve into serving portions and spoon over the cooking juices and garlic. Serve with boiled potatoes and a green salad and, most importantly, lots of crusty bread to mop up the juices and to spread with the creamy garlic.

Poulet en fricassée aux écrevisses
Chicken casserole and freshwater crayfish

Serves 4

This unusual combination of poultry and crustaceans is not your regular 'surf & turf'. Freshwater crayfish—otherwise known as crawfish or yabbies—do not have the strong briny flavour of their sea-dwelling cousins. Their rather earthy undertones marry beautifully with the chicken, rather than act as a contrast. Serve the dish with a pilaf and haricots vert.

24 FRESHWATER CRAYFISH

1 X 1.5KG (3LB 5OZ) CHICKEN

30G (1OZ) FLOUR, SEASONED WITH
  SALT AND PEPPER

50G (1¾OZ) BUTTER

1 CARROT, CHOPPED

1 ONION, CHOPPED

1 STICK CELERY, CHOPPED

4 CLOVES GARLIC, SLICED

SAUCE

2 TABLESPOONS OLIVE OIL

6 SHALLOTS (ESCHALOTS), CHOPPED

2 CLOVES GARLIC, SLICED

RESERVED CRAYFISH HEADS (SEE
  METHOD)

2 TABLESPOONS COGNAC

500 ML (16FL OZ/2 CUPS) WHITE
  WINE

6 TOMATOES, CHOPPED

1 BAY LEAF

4 SPRIGS TARRAGON

2 SPRIGS THYME

125M (4FL OZ/½ CUP) CREAM

SALT AND PEPPER

Preheat the oven to 180°C (350°F).

To prepare the crayfish, plunge into salted boiling water. Cook for 1 minute. Remove from the water and immediately plunge them into iced water to arrest the cooking. Once cold, remove the heads and set aside for the sauce. De-shell the bodies and remove the digestive tract, discard. Set aside the crayfish flesh.

Using a heavy cook's knife or kitchen shears split the chicken in half lengthways. Separate the legs from the carcass, then cut into thigh and drumstick pieces. Cut the remaining breast sections in half through the mid-section. You will have 8 pieces.

Dry off the chicken with a paper towel and then toss in seasoned flour. Heat the butter in a casserole gently, add the chicken and cook on all sides without colouring. Remove from the casserole and set aside. Add the carrot, onion, celery and garlic to the casserole and cook gently until translucent. Return the chicken to the casserole, cover and place in the heated oven for about 1 hour, until juices run clear. Remove the chicken from the casserole and set aside in a warm place. Discard the vegetables.

To prepare the sauce, heat the olive oil in the casserole. Add the shallots and garlic and fry gently until lightly coloured. Cut the reserved crayfish heads into 2.5-cm (1-in) pieces, add to the casserole and cook until they turn a vibrant red. Pour in the cognac and flambé by lighting; stand back and wait until the flames have subsided. Then add the wine, tomatoes and herbs. Bring to the boil and reduce the volume by half. Pour in the cream and continue to cook at a gentle simmer for 5 minutes. Strain the sauce through a fine mesh sieve, pressing firmly to extract as much of the precious liquid as possible. Adjust seasoning.

Return the sauce to a clean pan. Add the cooked chicken and crayfish. On a low flame, bring slowly to a simmer to reheat the chicken and finish cooking the crayfish.

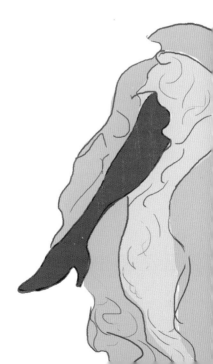

Lapin aux pruneaux
Rabbit casserole with prunes

Serves 4

The French regard rabbits as poultry because of the similarities in the meat, and think that most chicken recipes can be applied to them. I dispute this, as rabbit definitely has its own characteristic musky flavour.

Serve the dish with a pilaf or potato puree.

1 TABLESPOON BLACK TEA LEAVES

350G (12OZ) PITTED PRUNES

1 X 1.5KG (3LB 5OZ) RABBIT, WITH
    LIVER AND KIDNEYS IF POSSIBLE

1 TABLESPOON FLOUR

2 TABLESPOONS BUTTER

90G (3OZ) THICK FATTY BACON, CUT
    INTO LARDONS

16 PEARL ONIONS

250G (9OZ) CHAMPIGNONS

½ BUNCH THYME, CHOPPED

1 BOUQUET GARNI

750ML (24FLOZ/3 CUPS) RED WINE

1 TABLESPOON REDCURRANT JELLY

1 TABLESPOON BALSAMIC VINEGAR

SALT AND PEPPER

Make a strong brew of your favourite tea with tea leaves and boiling water. Pour it over the prunes and leave them to soak for 1 hour (the bergamot in Earl Grey leaves citrus notes).

If available, mince the rabbit liver and set aside. Cut the rabbit into 8 pieces: 2 forequarter legs, 2 back legs and the saddle cut through the bone into 4 pieces. Toss in the flour.

In a casserole heat the butter and fry the lardons and onions until crisp and golden. Remove with a slotted spoon and reserve. In the fat remaining in the casserole fry the rabbit until golden on all sides. Add the mushrooms, thyme, bouquet garni and wine. Bring to the boil and simmer for 30 minutes. Add the drained prunes, onions and lardons. Cook for a further 15 minutes. Discard the bouquet garni. Add the redcurrant jelly, vinegar and minced liver if using. Simmer for a further 5 minutes. Adjust seasoning and serve.

Les accompagnements
Side dishes

Pommes frites
à la graisse de canard
Potatoes fried in duck fat

Serves 4

These will be the most decadent 'chips' you have ever tasted. Duck fat imparts a rich butteriness that you don't get from other oils. Choose a low sugar, floury potato such as sebago or spunta.

1KG (2LB 4OZ) POTATOES, PEELED
1.5 LITRES (70FL OZ/6 CUPS) DUCK FAT
SALT

Cut the potatoes into 15-mm (⅔-in) batons. Dry on paper towels. Heat the fat in a deep-fryer or large saucepan to 140°C (275°F). In small batches, fry the potatoes for about 3 minutes, until cooked but not coloured. Increase the fat temperature to 180°C (350°F) and repeat the frying process until crisp and golden. Drain on paper towels, toss with salt and serve immediately.

Pommes purée
Mashed potatoes

Serves 4

There are many different ways to make mash, and most people will argue that they make the best. For me, baking the potatoes gives the best result—it drys out the potato and lets the flavour of the baked skin permeate the flesh. The drier flesh absorbs more cream and butter, giving a richer, glossier mash. Use a 'mealy' potato such as desiree or russet.

1KG (2LB 4OZ) POTATOES
200G (7OZ) BUTTER
250ML (8FL OZ/1 CUP) CREAM
½ TABLESPOON SALT
GROUND WHITE PEPPER

Preheat the oven to 180°C (350°F). Place the potatoes on a rack in the oven and bake for about 1 hour until well cooked. Heat the butter and cream in a saucepan until hot but not boiled. Cut the potatoes in half and scoop out the flesh. Puree through a mouli into a clean saucepan and beat in enough of the cream mix to get the required consistency. Taste and season.

VARIATION

Aligot

Cheese-enriched mash

This is mash on steroids. Using the pommes puree recipe, reduce the amount of butter to 60g (2oz) and add 300g (10oz) of grated Tomme (a French-Swiss alpine cheese) or use Gruyère. Proceed as for the usual recipe but once all ingredients are incorporated cook on a low heat stirring constantly until the mix forms an elastic-string texture. Serve hot.

Riz pilaf
Baked rice

Serves 4

An easy way to remember this method is that you use twice the amount of liquid to rice. Other flavourings such as saffron may be added to this basic recipe. For best results use a fragrant long-grain rice.

30G (1OZ) BUTTER

1 SMALL ONION, FINELY DICED

300G (10½OZ) LONG-GRAIN RICE

3 CUPS CHICKEN STOCK, HEATED

1 BAY LEAF

SALT AND PEPPER

Preheat the oven to 200°C (400°F). Melt the butter in a ovenproof saucepan. Add the onion and sautè until soft but not coloured. Add the rice and cook for another minute until all the rice grains are coated with the onion mix. Pour in the hot stock, add the bay leaf and season. Bring to the boil, stirring so that none of the rice catches on the bottom. Cover and bake for 20 minutes.

Remove from the oven and leave uncovered until most of the steam dissipates. Fluff up with a fork and serve.

Pommes lyonnaise
Sautéed potatoes with caramelised onions

Serves 4

*When a dish is described as 'lyonnaise' it almost always contains onions as its prime
ingredient. This dish, of course, goes well with the region's favourite offal and rich
wine-based dishes. Waxy potatoes such as kipfler are best to use, as they are less likely
to break up.*

500G (17½OZ) POTATOES
60G (2OZ) BUTTER
2 ONIONS, SLICED
2 SPRIGS THYME, CHOPPED
SALT AND PEPPER

Wash the potatoes well with a scouring pad to remove all dirt. Place them
in a saucepan and cover with cold water. Bring to the boil and simmer for
15 minutes. Drain and leave to cool in a colander. Once cool enough to handle,
scrape off the skins using a paring knife. Leave to cool completely. Cut the
potatoes into 1-cm (½-in) slices.

Heat the butter in a heavy-based frying pan and add the potato slices. Cook
until golden brown on all sides. Remove the potatoes from the pan and set aside.

Add the onions to the pan and cook slowly until golden and caramelised.
Return the potatoes to the pan and mix gently with the onions until the
potatoes are warmed through. Season and sprinkle with thyme.

Pommes dauphinoise
Potato gratin

Serves 4

The combination of potato, cream and garlic when baked in this fashion gives the dish its characteristic cheesy flavour. If you want a richer and cheesier flavour top it with a cup of grated Gruyère before baking.

750G (1LB 10OZ) POTATOES, PEELED
1 TABLESPOON BUTTER
250ML (8FL OZ/1 CUP) CREAM
½ CLOVE GARLIC
PINCH OF NUTMEG
1 TEASPOON THYME, CHOPPED
SALT AND PEPPER

Preheat the oven to 180°C (350°F). Slice the potatoes very thinly (about 2mm/⅛in thick). Do not wash at this stage—the starch is important as a binding agent. Grease a gratin dish with the butter. Mix the potatoes together with the rest of the ingredients and arrange in layers in the dish.

Bake in the heated oven for about 1 hour, until crisp and golden. Serve.

Gratin aux petits pois
Garlic-crusted pea puree

Serves 4

This is a take on a petit pois a la Français.

1 BUNCH SPRING ONIONS (SCALLIONS)
2 TABLESPOONS BUTTER
1 HEAD BABY COS LETTUCE, SHREDDED
200G (7OZ) GREEN PEAS
4 SLICES WHITE BREAD
2 CLOVES GARLIC
1 TEASPOON THYME, CHOPPED
SALT AND PEPPER

Preheat the oven to 200°C (400°F). Trim off the green parts from the spring onions and finely slice the bulbs. Heat the butter in a saucepan and cook the spring onions and lettuce until translucent. Meanwhile, cook the peas in boiling salted water until tender. Combine the onions, lettuce and peas in a food processor and pulse until you have a coarse puree. Season. Spread the puree into gratin dishes.

Cut the crusts from the bread and combine with the garlic and thyme in a food processor. Process until you have a fine crumb. Spread a layer over the pea puree and bake in the oven for 15 minutes until golden and crisp.

Choux de bruxelles à l'auvergnate
Pan-fried brussels sprouts with chestnuts

Serves 4

Brussels sprouts are one of my favourite vegetables. This dish is sure to convert the disbelievers. Use the smallest sprouts you can find.

350G (12OZ) BRUSSELS SPROUTS
60G (2OZ) BUTTER
100G (3½OZ) THICK BACON STRIPS, INCLUDING FAT (LARDONS)
1 SHALLOT (ESCHALOT), CHOPPED
2 CLOVES GARLIC, CRUSHED
16 CHESTNUTS, ROASTED AND PEELED
1 TABLESPOON SAGE LEAVES, SHREDDED
SALT AND PEPPER

Remove any discoloured leaves and cut an 'X' into the base of each brussels sprout so they cook evenly. Plunge them into salted boiling water and cook until tender.

Melt the butter in a frying pan and add the lardons. Fry until crisp and golden. Add in the shallot and garlic and fry briefly until softened. Add in the chestnuts and sage, tossing to warm through the chestnuts. Add the drained brussels sprouts, season and mix well.

Chou-fleur à la polonaise
Cauliflower with crisp breadcrumbs and egg

Serves 4

The crisp, garlicky breadcrumb and sieved egg topping gives a visual lift and flavour boost to this highly underrated vegetable. Use the same topping with boiled white or green asparagus.

1 EGG

1 HEAD CAULIFLOWER, SEPARATED INTO FLORETS

40G (1½OZ) FRESH BREADCRUMBS

1 CLOVE GARLIC

4 TABLESPOONS PARSLEY, CHOPPED

4 TABLESPOPONS BUTTER

PINCH OF NUTMEG

SALT AND PEPPER

Cook the egg in boiling water for 10 minutes. Cool and remove shell. Set aside. Cook the cauliflower florets in boiling salted water until tender, then drain and arrange in a serving dish.

In a food processor, combine the breadcrumbs, garlic and parsley and process until you have a vibrant green crumb. Melt the butter in a heavy-based frying pan. Add the nutmeg and cook until the butter becomes slightly coloured and nutty. Add the breadcrumb mixture, tossing it through the butter, and cook until toasted. Spoon this immediately over the cauliflower. Finish by topping with the egg forced through a sieve. Season and serve immediately.

Purée de carottes et cumin
Carrot and cumin puree

Serves 4

Naturally sweet carrots are the perfect accompaniment to balance out rich red wine-driven dishes. Don't peel the carrots for a stronger carrot flavour.

500G (17½OZ) CARROTS
100G (3½OZ) BUTTER
1 TEASPOON CUMIN SEEDS
SALT AND PEPPER

Wash and cut the tops from the carrots. Cut into even slices. Place in a saucepan and cover with cold water. Add the butter and bring to the boil. Cook on a medium heat with the lid askew for about 1 hour, until the carrots are meltingly tender and the liquid has reduced by half. Cool slightly. Toast the cumin seeds in a dry frying pan. Grind in a spice mill or a blender to a fine powder. Add the cooked carrots to the blender jar and process until you have a fine puree. Taste and adjust the seasoning.

Carottes Vichy
Glazed carrots

Serves 4

Named after the famous mineral water spring in Massif Central, in theory this dish should be cooked in Vichy water—but you will be forgiven if you use basic tap water. Use small heirloom or Dutch carrots simply scraped clean for the best flavour.

500G (17½OZ) CARROTS
250ML (8FL OZ/1 CUP) WATER
30G (1OZ) BUTTER
1 TEASPOON SUGAR
SALT AND PEPPER

Scrape clean and trim the greens from the carrots. Wash thoroughly.

Combine all the ingredients in a saucepan, cover and cook over low heat until tender. Remove the lid and increase the heat, stirring occasionally, until all the liquid has evaporated and the butter and sugar has formed a light glaze. Adjust the seasoning and serve.

Haricots verts aux échalotes
Green beans with shallots

Serves 4

This simple recipe calls for young tender beans, which are crackling fresh. They are tossed in flavoured oil to add a savoury note.

2 SHALLOTS (ESCHALOTS), CHOPPED
4 TABLESPOONS OLIVE OIL
250G (9OZ) GREEN BEANS
SALT AND PEPPER

Combine the shallots and olive oil in a saucepan. Bring slowly up to heat and cook until the shallots are soft and caramelised. Remove from the heat.

Cut the stalk end from the beans and cook in boiling salted water until tender. Drain well.

Mix together the beans and dressing while still warm. Season and serve.

Endives braisées
Braised witlof

Serves 4

This method of cooking uses a caramel that adds sweetness to counteract the witlof's bitterness.

2 TABLESPOONS SUGAR

30G (1OZ) BUTTER

4 HEADS OF WITLOF

JUICE OF 1 ORANGE

1 ORANGE, QUARTERED

2 THYME SPRIGS

1 BAY LEAF

SALT AND PEPPER

Preheat the oven to 180°C (350°F). In a heavy-based frying pan cook the sugar over a high heat until it melts and then caramelises. Add the butter, mixing well to form a kind of butterscotch. Turn the heat down to medium and add the witlof, turning frequently until lightly browned all over. Squeeze the orange juice into the pan to deglaze. Remove the pan from the heat and add the orange quarters and the herbs. Season to taste.

Cover the pan with foil and bake in the oven for 1 hour. Remove the herbs and serve.

Artichauts à la barigoule
Artichokes stuffed with mushrooms

Serves 4

Traditionally, this dish contained minced pork. It is believed that barigoule is a term adapted from the Provençal word farigoule, meaning thyme. Serve these hot or cold.

8 ARTICHOKES, MEDIUM SIZED

1 LEMON, HALVED

½ CELERY HEART

1 ONION, SLICED

½ CARROT, FINELY SLICED

½ BUNCH THYME

2 CLOVES GARLIC, SLICED

½ TEASPOON FENNEL SEEDS

½ TEASPOON CORIANDER SEEDS

1 BAY LEAF

250ML (8FL OZ/1 CUP) WHITE WINE

STUFFING

500G (17½OZ) BUTTON MUSHROOMS, FINELY CHOPPED

1 SHALLOT (ESCHALOT), FINELY CHOPPED

2 TABLESPOONS OLIVE OIL

40G (1½OZ) FRESH BREADCRUMBS

1 EGG

1 TABLESPOON PARSLEY, CHOPPED

SALT AND PEPPER

BUTCHERS' TWINE

Preheat the oven to 180°C (350°F). Trim the artichoke stems down to 5cm (2in). With a vegetable peeler, shave off the fibrous part leaving the fleshy stem. Cut the top quarter off the artichoke and break off all the woody leaves. Rub the cut surfaces with half the lemon to prevent discoloration. Blanch artichokes in a pan of salted water for 10 minutes. Remove and, once cooled, scoop out the 'choke' and discard.

For the stuffing, heat the oil in a pan and add the mushrooms and shallot. Sauté on a medium heat until lightly coloured and all the moisture has evaporated. Once cooled add the breadcrumbs, egg and parsley. Mix well and season. Fill the cavity of each artichoke with the mushroom mixture. Fold back in the leaves to encase the mix and secure with twine. Place the artichokes in a casserole with the remaining ingredients. Barely cover with water. Bring to a gentle simmer, then cover with a piece of greaseproof paper (to allow some evaporation but protect from the direct heat) and place in a oven for about 45 minutes, until tender.

To serve, remove twine from artichokes and spoon over some cooking liquid.

Ratatouille
Stewed Provençal vegetables

Serves 4

This is a great accompaniment to most meat and fish dishes. Make extra as it's equally good cold as an hors d'oeuvre.

750G (1LB 10OZ) TOMATOES, PEELED, SEEDED AND ROUGHLY CHOPPED
500G (17½OZ) EGGPLANT (AUBERGINE)
500G (17½OZ) ZUCCHINI (COURGETTES)
500G (17½OZ) GREEN CAPSICUMS (BELL PEPPERS)

500G (17½OZ) ONIONS
160ML (5¾FL OZ/⅔ CUP) OLIVE OIL
4 CLOVES GARLIC, CRUSHED
1 BOUQUET GARNI
10 BASIL LEAVES, SHREDDED
SALT AND PEPPER

Place the tomatoes in a sieve to drain.

Cut the eggplant, zucchini, capsicums and onions into 1-cm (½-in) slices. Set aside, keeping them separate.

In a saucepan heat 3 tablespoons of the oil and fry the onion until slightly coloured. Add the garlic and continue cooking for another 3 minutes. Add the drained tomatoes and bouquet garni and cook gently until you have a thick sauce.

While the sauce is cooking, in a frying pan brown the eggplant slices in 3 tablespoons of oil. Set aside. Repeat the process with the zucchini and then the capsicum in the remaining oil. Once the vegetables are done, transfer them in alternating layers into a casserole. Discard the bouquet garni and pour the sauce over the vegetables and stir gently. Simmer on a low heat for 15 minutes. Adjust seasoning. Scatter over the shredded basil leaves and serve.

Céleris braisés
Braised celery

Serves 4

Cooked celery can be a little insipid. This method of braising using stock permeates and enriches the vegetable so it is good enough to eat as a lunch dish on its own. Cut off the stalky green parts for another use—the yellow densely packed hearts are the best part.

2 HEADS CELERY
30G (1OZ) BUTTER
2 ONIONS, CHOPPED
1 CARROT, CHOPPED
3 CLOVES GARLIC
½ BUNCH THYME
1 BAY LEAF
500ML (16FL OZ/2 CUPS) BEEF STOCK
SALT AND PEPPER

Preheat the oven to 180°C (350°F). Trim off the green parts from the celery heads. Spilt the heads lengthways and wash very thoroughly in several changes of water to remove all sand and grit.

In a casserole melt the butter and then add the celery, cut side down, and cook until golden. Remove the celery and add the onion, carrot and garlic and cook until golden. Return the celery to the casserole along with the thyme, bay leaf and stock. Cover and cook in the heated oven for 1½ hours, until meltingly tender.

Remove the celery from the casserole and keep warm. Strain the cooking liquid through a sieve into a clean saucepan and reduce to make a sauce. Adjust the seasoning and spoon the sauce over the celery. Serve.

Chou rouge au vin
Red cabbage braised in wine

Serves 4–6

The red wine, tart apples and astringent vinegar make this the perfect side dish to offset the richness of pork, duck or game meats.

I RED CABBAGE, QUARTERED

30G (1OZ) BUTTER

I ONION, SLICED

500ML (16FL OZ/2 CUPS) RED WINE

2 TABLESPOONS RED WINE VINEGAR

I BAY LEAF

3 JUNIPER BERRIES, CRUSHED

¼ TEASPOON NUTMEG OR MACE

2 GRANNY SMITH APPLES, CORED AND CUT INTO LARGE CHUNKS

SALT AND PEPPER

Remove and discard the core from the cabbage, and slice very thinly.

Heat the butter in a casserole, add the onion and cook until translucent. Add the cabbage and cook until slightly collapsed. Pour in the wine, vinegar, bay leaf, juniper berries and nutmeg. Bring to the boil, and then add the apples. Cover with a piece of greaseproof paper (to allow some evaporation but protect from direct heat) and cook on a low heat for 1 hour, stirring occasionally. Discard the bay leaf and adjust the seasoning.

Concombres sautés
Sautéed cucumbers

Serves 4

Cooked cucumbers may not be to everyone's taste. But I promise you they make a spectacular accompaniment to fish dishes or white braises such as poached salmon or blanquette de veau. Be sure to cook them only briefly to retain colour and crunch.

2 TELEGRAPH CUCUMBERS, HALVED LENGTHWAYS

1 TABLESPOON OLIVE OIL

1 TABLESPOON BUTTER

1 SHALLOT (ESCHALOT), CHOPPED

½ TEASPOON SUGAR

1 TEASPOON CHERVIL, CHOPPED

1 TABLESPOON PARSLEY, CHOPPED

SALT AND PEPPER

Using a teaspoon, remove the seeds from the cucumber halves, then cut into 5cm- (2in-) long batons. Sprinkle them with a little salt and mix to distribute evenly. Place the cucumber in a colander and leave for half an hour to drain. Rinse to remove the salt and pat dry.

Over a medium heat, add the oil and butter to a frying pan, then add the cucumbers. Cook, tossing all time, until they are lightly coloured. Add the shallot and sugar and continue to cook until the cucumbers are glazed. Remove from the heat and mix through the chopped herbs. Adjust the seasoning and serve.

Fromage
Cheese

A meal without cheese in France is unthinkable, either as its own course following the main dish or as the ingredient in savoury or sweet dishes.

The holy trinity: cheese, bread, wine

I prefer to serve cheese without all the surplus garnish of fruit preserves and flavoured crackers. A well-made cheese is a masterpiece best savoured with neutral-flavoured bread and little else. If you wish to serve it with accompaniments, choose them as carefully as you would a wine—to complement and enhance the cheese. Below are some suggestions and wine matches.

Types of cheese

The origin of cheese is thought to have come about in ancient times, when nomads stored their milk in saddle bags made from the stomachs of young animals during their long journeys. The combination of the motion of the horse, the warmth from the sun and the natural coagulating enzyme present in the 'stomach' saddlebag curdled the milk. Undeterred by this, the travellers found they had a drinkable liquid and a crude cheese. This simple process is the basis of modern day cheese production.

All cheeses are formed with the process of coagulation. The milk is broken down into the solids (curds) and liquid (whey). A starter culture is added to warmed pasterurised milk to activate the splitting (pasteurisation destroys most naturally occurring good bacteria). Raw milk retains these bacteria, which coagulate to milk naturally. The results are the same but the myriad of flavour characteristics created by the natural bacteria cannot be replicated—which is why many French cheesemakers are very reluctant to use pasteurised milk and have defied European Union regulations.

Cheese formed after coagulation is sharp and acidic. Rennet, an enzyme present in milk-fed animals, is added to break down the curds, a process that vastly improves the texture and flavour. Plant-based enzymes are used in vegetarian cheeses.

Most cheeses are made using this method. It is how the curds are handled and what proportion of whey is retained that determine which of the six categories they can be loosely broken down into:

FRESH: This is simply fresh unripened curd. Fresh cheeses are uncomplicated, uncooked and high in moisture. They retain the pure essence of the milk from which they are made. Examples are fromage blanc, feta, fromage frais.

Serve fresh cheese simply on toast with a grassy cold-pressed olive oil, which will reinforce the freshness of a fresh cheese. These cheeses also benefit from a burst of piquancy from such condiments as tapenade. In cooking fresh cheeses are a useful vehicle to carry flavours—their neutrality provides a soft background note to introduced flavourings, as in the tarte au fromage blanc below.

A crisp fruity white wine such as a sauvignon blanc is best suited to this style.

Tarte au fromage blanc

I X QUANTITY OF PATE SUCRÉE (SEE PAGE 227)

3 EGGS, SEPARATED

ZEST OF I LEMON

I VANILLA BEAN

IKG (2LB 4OZ) FROMAGE BLANC

80G (2½OZ) SUGAR

Preheat the oven to 180°C (350°F). Butter and flour a 22-cm (9-in) tart mould. Line with the rolled pastry. Refrigerate for 30 minutes to rest. Once firm, trim off the excess pastry.

Beat the egg yolks in a mixing bowl until light and pale. Add the grated lemon zest, the seeds scraped from a split vanilla pod and the cheese. Mix until smooth. In a separate bowl, whisk the egg whites to form soft peaks, then gradually whisk in the sugar until the whites are stiff and glossy. Gently fold the egg whites into the cheese mixture, making sure the mix is smooth and homogenous.

Pour into the prepared tart shell. Bake for 40–50 minutes, until the tart is risen and browned. Leave to cool slightly before unmoulding. Serve warm or cold with seasonal fruit. This is particularly good with fresh berries or stone fruit. *Serves 8*

WHITE MOULD: These are surface-ripened fresh cheeses—they have had a white mould culture added, which encases the cheese, preserving it. As the cheese ripens, the mould breaks down the proteins in the curd, converting the chalky interior into a soft pâté. The white mould culture is much like any other fungi and permeates the cheese with a mushroom flavour. Examples are Brie de Meaux, Brillat-Savarin and Camembert de Normandie.

White mould cheeses are made to be served as table cheeses, and are rarely used in cooking. However natural rind cheeses are a sub-category and are well suited for melting and grilling (for example, in salade de chevre chaud).

Buttery chardonnay pairs well with stronger meaty white moulds; milder varieties require a chenin blanc or vouvray. A light pinot noir is also a good pairing, especially with natural rinded goat's cheeses.

WASHED RIND: Washed rind cheeses are surface ripened. Instead of a mould being introduced, the growth of bacteria is promoted through the washing of the curd in a bath of brine, wine or other alcohols. The resulting finish is usually a sticky orange rind with a meltingly soft centre. The flavours are complex, ranging from nutty to yeasty and meaty. A word of warning to those unfamiliar to this variety: they can be described as pungent. In fact they were once banned from French public transport! Examples of a washed rind cheese are Pont l'Eveque, Munster, and Reblochon.

They are best used to flavour bland dishes such as polenta and risottos. When served as a table cheese, grapes or pears are a good counterbalance to their piquancy and spiciness.

It is not uncommon to serve them with a rich yeasty beer. The milder washed rind cheeses match gewürztraminer; the stronger flavoured ones can handle robust reds such as grenache.

BLUE: Blue cheeses are unlike any other cheese variety, as they ripen from the centre. The curds are treated with blue mould spores, then loosely packed in hoops to drain off excess whey under their own weight. This method retains moisture and traps air. Once they are able to support their own weight, the cheeses are unmoulded and salted. Although the cheese have been infected with the mould spores, they will not turn blue until pierced, which allows in enough air for the mould to flourish. Most blue cheeses are characteristically sharp, salty and tangy. Examples are Roquefort, Fourme d'Ambert and Bleu d'Auvergne.

Blue cheeses are best suited as table cheese, showing off their dramatic cracked porcelain veining, but also work well to lift a salad (salade Roquefort, page 84) or to complement rich meats such as steaks or duck. Whatever the application the blue cheese will always be the star. On the cheeseboard, honeycomb is the prefect partner for the sharp, salty bite of blue cheese.

As a rule, sweet wines are the perfect partner for blue cheeses. A mild variety pairs well with a rosé or chenin blanc; stronger blues require the sticky sweetness of a fortified or dessert wine. Roquefort with Sauternes is a classic combination.

Sauce Roquefort

2 SHALLOTS (ESCHALOTS), CHOPPED
1 TABLESPOON BUTTER
4 TABLESPOONS PORT
125MI (4FL OZ/½ CUP) BEEF STOCK
125MI (4FL OZ/½ CUP) CREAM
100G (3½OZ) ROQUEFORT

Melt the butter in a saucepan, then add the shallots and sauté until a light golden brown. Pour in the port. Reduce until it is the consistency of a thick glaze. Add the beef stock and reduce by half. Pour in the cream. Bring to a simmer and then turn off the heat. Crumble in the Roquefort and stir gently to amalgamate (but leave some of the cheese in lumps for texture). Serve immediately. *Makes 250ml (1 cup/8fl oz)*

SEMI-HARD: The firm texture of a semi-hard cheese is achieved by cutting the curd to release some of the whey. The curd is then pressed into moulds to extract more of the whey. The cheeses are brined to seal the rind and then cellared to mature—the length of cellaring will determne their flavour, texture and the rind formation. Examples are Morbier, Raclette and Ossau-Iraty.

These cheeses tend to be well rounded and flavourful and are most at home in the kitchen and used for cooking. When cooked, they melt and produce long glossy elastic strands. Classic 'gratin' dishes usually call for this style of cheese.

Dried muscatels or freshly shelled nuts are good served with semi-hard table cheeses, and quince paste goes particularly well, especially with those made from sheep's or goat's milk.

Pinot noir is a good wine to serve. Try a merlot or shiraz with stronger more complex cheeses.

HARD: Hard cheeses are made by the same process as semi-hard ones ut the emphasis on extracting most of the whey. The curds are cooked and cut finer to facilitate this extraction. The curds are then salted or formed into a cheese and brined to encourage a rind. Cheeses in this style may be allowed to age for months or years. Well-aged hard cheeses have a crumbly texture, robust flavour and are slightly sweet with flourishes of salt crystals. Most of us are familiar with the cheddar-style cheeses, which encompass much of this variety and can range from a young milky sweetness to a more acidic sharp older cheese. Examples are Mimolette, Cantal and Beaufort.

Fresh apples or figs are best with young cheese and the condensed flavours of dried fruit with aged ones.

The flavour profiles of these varieties of cheeses vary greatly, making this the most challenging to match to wine. The maturing process is a major factor to consider. The cheeses will change in both texture and taste considerably as moisture is lost and flavours concentrate. Eat young cheeses with young fruity reds, and aged cheeses with a well matured cheeses.

Les desserts
Sweet things

Fruits en saison
Seasonal fruits

Dessert need not be a an elaborate affair. Offering fruits at their peak with little more than a dusting of powdered sugar and crème chantilly is common. Here are two of the most widely known. Also try cherries in late summer or citrus fruits in winter with a dash of Grand Marnier and candied angelica.

Ananas au kirsch
Pineapple with cherry brandy

1 PINEAPPLE
4 TABLESPOONS KIRSCH
20 DRIED SOUR CHERRIES

Peel and core the pineapple. Cut into wedges. Drizzle over the kirsch and leave to macerate for a few minutes. Arrange on serving plates and scatter over the cherries. Serve with crème chantilly.

Fraises ou framboises au sucre
Strawberries or raspberries with sugar

2 PUNNETS STRAWBERRIES OR RASPBERRIES
1 TABLESPOON ICING SUGAR

Wash and dry the fruit. Arrange in chilled dessert coupes. Dust with icing sugar and serve with crème chantilly.

Crème chantilly

1 VANILLA POD
250ML (8FL OZ/1 CUP) WHIPPING CREAM
2 TABLESPOONS CASTER SUGAR

Split the vanilla pod lengthways. Scrape out the seeds. Combine the vanilla seeds, cream and sugar in a bowl and whisk until soft peaks form.

Crème brûlée
Caramelised vanilla custard

Serves 4

No bistro would be complete without this classic—a rich silken-smooth custard perfumed with vanilla, under a layer of crisp caramel begging to be released with the crack from the back of a spoon.

1 VANILLA POD
500ML (16FL OZ/2 CUPS) CREAM
5 EGG YOLKS
75G (2½OZ) CASTER SUGAR
DEMERARA SUGAR FOR CARAMEL

Preheat the oven to 120°C (225°F). Cut the vanilla pod lengthways, scrape out the seeds and add them and the pod to a saucepan containing the cream. Heat gently to infuse the flavour into the liquid, but don't boil.

In a bowl, whisk together the yolks and caster sugar. Pour the cream onto the yolks and mix well. Pass through a fine sieve to remove the vanilla pod and any lumps. (The vanilla pod can be rinsed in water, dried and stored in sugar to give you vanilla-scented sugar.)

Pour the mix into an ovenproof dish or individual dishes (the larger the surface area, the more caramel is required). Cook in a bain-marie for about 1 hour, until set. Try to undercook it a little—the cooking process will continue after the crème is removed from the oven. Leave to cool. Store in fridge until needed (this may be up to a few days).

Just before serving, sprinkle the tops with demerara sugar and, using a blow torch, carefully caramelise the sugar to golden brown. This process can done under a grill but a blow torch gives you more control. Serve.

Tarte au citron
Lemon tart

Serves 8

A rich combination of crisp almond pastry and silky sweet and sour custard, this is the perfect end to a meal. This tart is best eaten on the day of baking while still warm.

6 EGGS, PLUS 5 YOLKS
225G (8OZ) CASTER SUGAR
GRATED ZEST OF 2 LEMONS
300ML (10FL OZ/1¼ CUPS) CREAM
150ML (4FL OZ) LEMON JUICE
1 QUANTITY OF PÂTÉ SUCRÉE (SEE RECIPE, PAGE 227)

Preheat the oven to 180°C (350°F). To make the lemon custard, gently whisk together the eggs, yolks, sugar and lemon zest. Don't whisk too vigorously or the mix will be over-aerated—just dissolve the sugar and release the oils from the zest. Mix cream and juice together, then add the egg mixture and stir through. Pass the mixture through a fine mesh sieve to remove the zest. Leave this to settle and skim off any foam that has risen to the surface.

Roll out the prepared pastry dough on a lightly floured surface. Lightly butter and flour a 25-cm (10-in) tart tin. Line the tin with the pastry, leaving a good amount of overhang. Blind bake the tart shell (place a round of baking paper and a layer of baking beans in the tin and bake for 30 minutes). Trim away the excess pastry from around the edge of the tin.

Reduce the oven to 140°C (275°F). Pour the lemon custard into the pastry shell and bake for about 45 minutes. The key to this dish is to undercook the custard slightly. If you move the tart gently and it has some give, much like a set jelly, then it's ready.

Leave to cool to room temperature, then slice and serve as is or with double cream. A dusting of icing sugar or icing sugar caramelised with a blow torch will hide any imperfections and add an extra dimension.

Pêche Melba
Poached peaches with ice cream and raspberries

Serves 4

This grand dish, created by the famous chef Auguste Escoffier as a tribute to the singer Dame Nellie Melba, has been simplified as it has become part of popular culture. Peaches and raspberries are an exquisite combination when at their peak in midsummer.

1 VANILLA POD, SPLIT
300G (10OZ) SUGAR
1 PUNNET FRESH RASPBERRIES
1 TABLESPOON ICING SUGAR
4 FRESH PEACHES
2 TABLESPOONS ALMOND SLIVERS, TOASTED
8 SCOOPS VANILLA ICE CREAM
4 TABLESPOONS CRÈME CHANTILLY (SEE PAGE 194)

Cut the vanilla pod lengthways, scrape out the seeds and add them and the pod to a saucepan with the sugar and 750ml (24floz/3 cups) of water into a saucepan. Bring to the boil to dissolve the sugar and infuse the vanilla. Take off the heat to cool.

Blend half the raspberries with the icing sugar. Pass through a fine sieve to obtain a smooth sauce; cool. Reserve the other raspberries for garnish.

Add the whole peaches to the cooled syrup. Cover with a piece of greaseproof paper. Bring to a gentle simmer, then take off the heat to cool. Chill in the refrigerator.

Cut the peaches in half, peel off the skins and remove the stones. Arrange, cut side up, in small chilled dessert bowls. Spoon over the raspberry sauce. Top each peach half with a scoop of vanilla ice cream and a spoon of crème chantilly. Scatter over the reserved raspberries and the slivered almonds.

Mousse au chocolat noir
Dark chocolate mousse

Serves 4

This is a velvety rich concoction, needing little more than a crunch of wafer or langues de chat. This recipe is for dark chocolate, preferably with no less than 60 per cent cocoa solids. Don't use milk or white chocolate—the setting characteristics are different.

220G (7½OZ) DARK CHOCOLATE
200G (7OZ) CREAM
6 EGG WHITES
60G (2OZ) SUGAR

Melt the chocolate in a bowl over a saucepan of hot water. Whip the cream in another bowl until soft peaks form. In a separate, scrupulously clean bowl whisk the egg whites to soft peaks, then gradually add in the sugar.

Fold the whipped cream through the chocolate. Be sure you add the cream to the chocolate; if you add the chocolate to the cold cream, the mixture will 'seize'. Once the cream and chocolate have been incorporated, fold through the beaten egg whites. Mix gently until you have a light homogenous mousse. Pour into serving dishes or glasses. Chill to set in the refrigerator.

Fondant au chocolat
Soft-centred chocolate pudding

Serves 6

The perfect fondant should have a rich, cakey exterior encasing a molten flowing interior. Essentially, it is an undercooked chocolate cake and it's all about timing. This recipe works in my oven, but the temperature of yours may be different. I suggest you have a trial run before that big dinner party or you may have a flop on your hands. At the restaurant I serve the fondant in coffee cups topped with a coffee 'foam'. This eliminates the need for turning the pudding out, which is the stressful part. The coffee foam is nothing more than a coffee-infused crème anglaise, which is aerated using a cream siphon.

4 EGGS, PLUS 2 YOLKS

1 CUP SUGAR

170G (6OZ) DARK CHOCOLATE

150G (5OZ) BUTTER, PLUS EXTRA FOR MOULDS

½ CUP COCOA, PLUS EXTRA FOR DUSTING

½ CUP FLOUR

Preheat the oven to 200°C (400°F). Beat together the eggs, yolks and sugar until pale and creamy.

Melt the chocolate and butter together, mixing occasionally until you have a glossy homogenous liquid. Add the egg mixture to the chocolate and combine well. Then sift in the cocoa and flour. Mix throughly to insure against lumps.

Butter six moulds and dust with cocoa. Fill to half way with the fondant mix.

Bake for 10 minutes. Carefully turn out onto serving plates, or serve in the moulds topped with foam (see above and photograph opposite) and dusted with cocoa. Serve with fresh berries and ice cream.

Clafoutis
Cherry gratin

Serves 4

This is a thick fruit pancake from Limousin, a region famous for small black cherries. When cherries are not in season other fruits are equally successful. Also try apricots or mulberries. My personal favourite is quince.

2 TABLESPOONS FLOUR

PINCH OF SALT

60G (2OZ) CASTER SUGAR

4 EGGS, PLUS 2 YOLKS

600ML (21FL OZ/2½ CUPS) MILK

1 TEASPOON ORANGE BLOSSOM WATER

BUTTER FOR DISH

500G (17½OZ) CHERRIES, PITTED

ICING SUGAR FOR DUSTING

VANILLA ICE CREAM TO SERVE

Preheat the oven to 190°C (375°F). Sift the flour and salt into a bowl. Add the sugar. Beat together the eggs, yolks, milk and orange blossom water. Gradually beat the egg mixture into the dry ingredients until just incorporated—overmixing will result in a tough batter.

Butter individual ovenproof dishes or a large dish and scatter over the cherries. Pass the batter through a fine sieve over the cherries. Bake in the heated oven for about 15 minutes for individual clafoutis and 45 minutes for a large one, until the clafoutis is golden brown and puffed.

Dust with icing sugar and serve with vanilla ice cream. The hot and cold contrast is outstanding.

Tarte aux pignons et agrumes
Pinenut and confit citrus tart

Serves 8

This tart is typical of Niçoise cooking. Pinenuts are usually seen in savoury dishes, most famously pesto. But throughout the Mediterranean they are commonly used in desserts and sweetmeats. Pinenuts are highly prized for their buttery texture and slight crunch. Serve the tart warm with crème anglaise or cold with honeyed fromage blanc.

300G (101/2OZ) GLACÉ ORANGES AND LEMONS, CHOPPED

3 TABLESPOONS GRAND MARNIER

150G (5OZ) BUTTER, ROOM TEMPERATURE

GRATED ZEST OF I ORANGE

125G (4OZ) SUGAR

3 EGGS

125G (4OZ) GROUND ALMONDS

I QUANTITY OF PÂTÉ SUCRÉE (SEE RECIPE, PAGE 227)

200G (7OZ) PINENUTS

Preheat the oven to 180°C (350°F). Macerate the glacé fruit in Grand Marnier for 1 hour. Beat together the butter, orange zest and sugar until light and pale. Beat in the eggs one at a time. Fold through the ground almonds and macerated glacé fruit. Pour the mixture into a tart mould lined with pâté sucre. Scatter over a layer of pinenuts. Bake in the heated oven for 20 minutes, then lower the oven temperature to 150°C (300°F) and bake for a further 30 minutes. Cool slightly before unmoulding.

Macarons de Mont Blanc
Chestnut cream macaroons

Serves 6

Macaroons are little almond petits four created in Nancy by nuns during the French Revolution. After being forced from their convent, they opened a bakery specialising in this crisp and deliciously chewy little cake. The popularity of macaroons is at an all-time high and an infinite variety of flavours and colours are popular. This version combines macaroons with the classic chestnut-flavoured dessert, Mont Blanc.

100G (3½OZ) ICING SUGAR
100G (3½OZ) ALMOND MEAL
2 EGG WHITES
75G (2½OZ) CASTER SUGAR
6 CANDIED CHESTNUTS (MARRONS GLACE)
COCOA FOR DUSTING

FILLING
150ML (⅔ CUP) CREAM
350G (12OZ) SWEETENED CHESTNUT PUREE (CRÈME DE MARRONS)

For the macaroons, combine the icing sugar and almond meal in a food processor. Blend together to a fine powder. Sift through a sieve into a bowl.

Whisk the egg whites until soft peaks form. Gradually add in the caster sugar, whisking vigorously until stiff peaks.

Add a third of the meringue to the almond mixture and, using a rubber spatula, gently combine together. Add in the remaining meringue. Fold through thoroughly until the mix is smooth and shiny. Transfer the macaroon mixture to a piping bag. Pipe 12 rounds onto trays lined with baking paper.

Leave the macaroons out on a bench for 1–2 hours, until not sticky to touch. Preheat the oven to 150°C (300°F). Bake for 18–20 minutes. The finished macaroons will have a thin crisp shell and soft moist interior. Once cool, carefully remove from the tray. you can store in an airtight container for up to 3 days.

To make the filling, whip the cream to soft peaks. Mix together a third of the cream with the chestnut puree. Transfer to a piping bag fitted with a superfine nozzle.

Lay out 6 macaroon shells and top with a spoon of the reserved whipped cream. Then pipe out the chestnut cream over the whipped cream so it looks like broken spaghetti. Decorate with halves of candied chestnuts. Top with the remaining macaroons and dust with cocoa.

Serve immediately. For an even more stunning presentation, top with gold leaf and piped chocolate.

Profiteroles glacées au chocolat
Choux puffs with vanilla ice cream and hot chocolate sauce

Serves 4

You are never too old for ice cream and hot chocolate sauce. This is the grown up version.

> 1 X QUANTITY CHOUX PASTRY (SEE RECIPE, PAGE 227)
> 1 X QUANTITY VANILLA ICE CREAM (SEE RECIPE, PAGE 222)
> 1 X QUANTITY HOT CHOCOLATE SAUCE (SEE BELOW)

Preheat the oven to 200°C (400°F). For the choux puffs, place walnut-sized pieces of choux pastry on a buttered baking sheet, well spaced from each other. Bake for 10 minutes, then reduce the temperature to 175°C (350°F) and cook for a further 20–25 minutes. Transfer to a wire rack to cool.

Once cooled, cut the puffs in half and fill with a scoop of vanilla ice cream. Drizzle over the hot chocolate sauce and serve.

Sauce au chocolat chaud
Hot chocolate sauce

> 75G (2½OZ) COCOA POWDER
> 150G (5OZ) SUGAR
> 30G (1OZ) BUTTER
> 100G (3½OZ) DARK CHOCOLATE, BROKEN UP

Combine the cocoa, sugar and 150 ml (⅔ cup/5fl oz) of water in a saucepan. Bring to the boil, whisking constantly. Take off the heat and whisk in the butter and chocolate. Keep warm until needed.

Savarins au rhum
Rum syrup cakes

Serves 4

The discovery of a new dish confers more happiness on humanity,
than the discovery of a new star. — *Jean-Anthelme Brillat-Savarin*

The famous gastronome may well have been speaking of the dish created in his honour by the Julien brothers in Paris. The savarin is a ring-shaped yeast gateau not unlike a doughnut, although a savarin is baked and a doughnut is deep-fried. After baking, the savarin is bathed in hot syrup and doused in rum. I like to serve it with thick slices of pineapple roasted with vanilla.

This dough is also the base for Babas au Rhum. Simply follow the same method but add 3 tablespoons of raisins macerated in 2 tablespoons of rum (at the stage when the butter is added) and bake in dariole moulds rather then savarin ones.

I TEASPOON DRY YEAST
125G (4OZ) FLOUR
I TABLESPOON SUGAR
PINCH OF SALT
I EGG
50G (1¾OZ) BUTTER, AT ROOM
  TEMPERATURE
100ML (2¾FL OZ/⅓ CUP) RUM
CRÈME CHANTILLY (SEE RECIPE,
  PAGE 194) TO SERVE

SAUCE CARAMEL AU BEURRE SALÉ
  (SEE RECIPE, PAGE 214)

SUGAR SYRUP
250G (9OZ) SUGAR
500ML (16FL OZ/2 CUPS) WATER
I VANILLA BEAN

Mix together the yeast and 1 tablespoon of tepid water and leave for 5 minutes. Butter and flour savarin moulds.

Combine the flour, sugar and salt in a mixing bowl. Add the yeast mixture and the egg. Mix together until you have smooth glossy dough. This will take about 5 minutes by hand or you could use an electric mixer. Work in the softened

CONTINUES ON PAGE 214

butter until amalgamated. The result will be very a very supple, silken dough. Transfer the dough to a piping bag and pipe into the prepared savarin moulds. Leave in a warm place until doubled in volume.

Preheat the oven to 200°C (375°F). Bake the savarins for 15–20 minutes until risen and golden. Remove from their moulds and leave to cool on a wire rack. At this stage the savarins may be kept in an airtight container for up to 5 days.

For the sugar syrup, combine the sugar, water and vanilla in a saucepan. Bring to the boil, then lower the heat and simmer for 5 minutes. Remove the syrup from the heat. Pour the syrup into a shallow bowl and add the savarins. Leave to soak until saturated. Carefully lift them out of the syrup with a slotted spoon and transfer to a wire rack. Drizzle over the rum.

Serve immediately with crème Chantilly and sauce caramel au beurre salé.

Sauce caramel au beurre salé
Salted caramel sauce

Makes 1 cup

A favourite of Brittany, this unusual-sounding combination of salt and sugar actually makes sense. The salt cuts the sweetness of the sugar and stimulates the taste buds, adding another dimension. As well as with the savarin, it is good served hot on ice cream or with crêpes.

250G (9OZ) SUGAR
250ML (8FL OZ/1 CUP) CREAM
30G (1OZ) BUTTER
¼ TEASPOON SALT (PREFERABLY FLEUR DE SEL)

Combine the sugar and ½ cup of water in a saucepan. On a high heat, stir to dissolve the sugar. Bring to the boil, and cook until you have a deep mahogany caramel.

Remove from the heat and stir in the cream, butter and salt. Whisk together to obtain a smooth homogenous sauce. Serve hot. The sauce can be refrigerated for up to 3 days and reheated.

Vacherin aux fruits de la passion
Passionfruit meringues

Serves 8

Freezing egg whites improves their foaming power and makes then easier to whip than fresh eggs. If you're not sure how many you've frozen, one tablespoon is roughly equivalent to one egg white. You can fill the meringues with crème Chantilly if you wish, although I prefer to serve them with ice cream. Decorate the vacherins with nasturtium flowers if you have them—they look beautiful and have a vibrant peppery flavour.

125ML(4FL OZ/½ CUP) EGG WHITES
125G (4OZ) CASTER SUGAR
100G (3½OZ) ICING SUGAR
1 TABLESPOON CORNFLOUR
1 TEASPOON ORANGE BLOSSOM
   WATER

½ TEASPOON GRATED ORANGE ZEST
8 SCOOPS VANILLA ICE CREAM
8 TABLESPOON CRÈME CHANTILLY
   (SEE RECIPE, PAGE 194)
8 PASSIONFRUIT
4 NASTURTIUM FLOWERS

Preheat the oven to 140°C (275°F).

Make sure the bowl and whisk are clean. Whisk the egg whites until soft peaks are achieved. Gradually add in the caster sugar, whisking vigorously until all the sugar has been incorporated and you have a thick glossy meringue.

Sift together the icing sugar and cornflour. Gently fold into the egg mixture along with the orange blossom water and orange zest.

Transfer the meringue to a piping bag. Line a baking tray with baking paper and pipe the meringue into eight 10-cm (2-in) disks.

Bake in the preheated oven for about 1½ hours, until the meringues have a crisp crust and soft centre. Transfer to a wire rack to cool.

To serve, place a meringue disk on each plate. Top with a scoop of ice cream and a tablespoon of crème Chantilly. Spoon over the pulp from a passionfruit. Aarrange the nasturtium flowers around the vacherins.

Canneles bordelais
Caramel rum cakes

Makes 12

These curious little cakes from Bordeaux have a thick chewy caramelised crust with a soft custardy centre. To achieve this crust the caneles are baked in their own special fluted moulds. Natural beeswax is usually used to line the moulds—this makes them easier to unmould and will not burn as butter or oil can—although I have used butter. If you want to use beeswax, make sure you use the untreated kind.

I VANILLA POD
500ML (16FL OZ/2 CUPS) MILK
200G (7OZ) SUGAR
2 EGGS, PLUS 2 YOLKS

90G (3OZ) BUTTER
125G (4OZ) FLOUR
2 TABLESPOONS RUM
2 DROPS BITTER ALMOND ESSENCE

Split the vanilla pod down the centre and scrape out the seeds. Combine the pod and seeds with the milk in a saucepan. Bring to a simmer and then let sit for 10 minutes.

Whisk together the sugar and the eggs and yolks. Pour on the infused milk. Mix well. Return this mixture to the saucepan and cook gently, stirring all the time. Bring to a simmer, then remove from the heat. (This is basically a split or overcooked crème anglaise.) Stir in half the butter.

Add the flour and whisk until you have a smooth batter. Cool, then add the rum and almond essence.

Cover and chill in the refrigerator for at least 24 hours, up to 3 days.

Preheat the oven to 200°C (400°F). Butter the moulds with the remaining butter. Fill the moulds three-quarter full.

Bake in the oven for 50–60 minutes, depending on how dark you like the cakes. They are done when a skewer comes out clean. Unmould immediately.

Serve straight from the oven or store in an airtight container for up to 5 days and refresh in a hot oven before serving.

Glace à la vanille
Vanilla ice cream

Makes about 1 litre (32fl oz/4 cups)

Ice cream is a frozen, aerated rich egg custard. This is a basic recipe and the flavour can be altered by adding additional ingredients—for instance, you can add chopped glacé fruit or nuts or change the spicing by infusing it into the milk.

2 VANILLA PODS
375ML (12FL OZ/1½ CUPS) MILK
9 EGG YOLKS
350G (12OZ) SUGAR
750ML (24FLOZ/3 CUPS) CREAM

Split the vanilla pod lengthways and scrape out the seeds. Put the seeds and pods in a saucepan with the milk. Bring to a simmer, then take off the heat and infuse for 30 minutes.

Whisk together the yolks and sugar until light and creamy. Pour on the infused milk. Mix well, then pour back into the saucepan. Cook over a very low heat, stirring continuously. Do not boil. The custard is done when it coats the back of a spoon and holds a line drawn in it. Strain the mixture through a sieve to remove the vanilla pods. Chill over ice to stop the cooking process. Pour in the cream and mix well.

Churn in an ice cream maker, according to the manufacturer's instructions.

Crème anglaise
Custard sauce

Makes 500ml (16fl oz/2 cups)

This is the basic recipe for vanilla custard. It is much the same process as ice cream, but contains less eggs. Use other spices such as cinnamon or nutmeg in place of the vanilla. A shot of your favourite spirit always works well too—adding it at the end of cooking. To make café anglaise, infuse ½ tablespoon of freshly ground coffee beans into the milk.

1 VANILLA POD
500ML (16FL OZ/2 CUPS) MILK
5 EGG YOLKS
60G (2OZ) SUGAR

Split the vanilla pod lengthways and scrape out the seeds. Put the seeds and pods with the milk in a saucepan and bring to a simmer. Take off the heat and leave to infuse for 30 minutes. In a bowl, whisk together the egg yolks and sugar until pale and creamy. Pour the infused milk onto the eggs and mix well.

Return the custard to the saucepan and cook on a very low heat, stirring continuously. Do not boil. The custard is done when it coats the back of a spoon and holds a line drawn in it. Strain the mixture through a sieve. Use immediately warm or chill over ice for cold preparations.

Le sabayon
Whipped fortified wine custard

Serves 4

A close cousin of the Italian zabaglione, the sabayon can be served as it is, chilled in glasses to accompany fresh figs. The French way is to spoon it over fresh fruit and glaze under a grill to add an extra dimension of flavour and interest.

4 EGG YOLKS
65G (2OZ) SUGAR
200ML (7FL OZ) PORT, MUSCAT OR SHERRY
FRESH OR POACHED FRUITS TO SERVE
ICING SUGAR TO SERVE

Whisk the yolks and sugar together until light and pale. Add the alcohol of choice. Place the bowl over a saucepan of simmering water and continue to whisk vigorously until the mixture thickens and is able to hold its shape. Take off the heat and continue to whisk until cooled.

Pour into glasses and chill in the refrigerator.

Alternatively, pour the sabayon over plates of prepared fruit—for example, fresh raspberries and apricots or poached rhubarb and pears. Place under a hot grill briefly, to form a light caramelised crust. Dust with icing sugar and serve the sabayon immediately.

Langues de chat
Cats' tongues

Makes 24

These thin crisp biscuits add crunch to desserts or can be served with coffee as petits fours. They are so named for their slightly rough texture and characteristic shape.

2 EGG WHITES
60G (2OZ) FLOUR
60G (2OZ) SUGAR
60G (2OZ) BUTTER, MELTED AND COOLED

Preheat the oven to 180°C (350°F). Whisk the egg whites until they just start to foam. Add the flour, sugar and cooled butter. Mix thoroughly until you have a thick, smooth, glossy batter.

Fill a piping bag fitted with a 5-mm (¼-in) round nozzle. Pipe 7-cm (3-in) lengths onto a buttered baking tray and bake for 10 minutes. The edges should be golden brown and the centres still quite pale.

Cool on a wire rack and store in an airtight container.

Pâte sucrée
Sweetcrust pastry

350G (12OZ) PLAIN FLOUR
150G (5OZ) GROUND ALMONDS
200G (7OZ) PURE ICING SUGAR
200G (7OZ) COLD BUTTER, CUT INTO SMALL CUBES
1 EGG, PLUS 3 YOLKS

Combine the flour, almonds, sugar and butter in a food processor and blend until the butter has been incorporated into the dry ingredients. Mix the egg and yolks together, then add to the processor and pulse until the mixture forms a ball. Do not overmix or the pastry will be tough and brittle. Wrap the dough in plastic film and rest in the refrigerator for about 1 hour before using. The pastry can be prepared the day before or frozen until needed.

Pâte à choux
Choux pastry

125ML (4FL OZ/½ CUP) MILK
125ML (4FL OZ/½ CUP) WATER
100G (3½OZ) BUTTER
⅛ TEASPOON SALT
1 TEASPOON SUGAR
150G (5OZ) FLOUR
4 EGGS

Put the milk, water, butter, salt and sugar into a pan and bring to a rapid boil. Tip in the flour, mixing vigorously to avoid lumps; keep mixing until the dough forms a ball. Cool slightly. Beat in the eggs one at a time, making sure each is fully incorporated before adding another. The finished pastry should be thick, smooth and glossy.

Les Menus

Le printemps
Spring

Salade Niçoise
(Niçoise salad)
Rosé

Gigot d'agneau aux flageolets
(Roast leg of lamb with
flageolet beans)
avec
Artichauts à la barigoule
(Artichokes stuffed with mushrooms)
Red Bordeaux

Tarte au citron
(Lemon tart)
Beaumes-de-Venise

L'été
Summer

Melon jambon
(Charentais melon with
ham & port)
Chardonnay or Pinot Gris

Thon aux tomates rôties
(Tuna steaks with roasted tomatoes)
avec
Concombres sautés
(Sautéed cucumbers)
Chardonnay or Pinot Gris

Pêche Melba
(Poached peach with vanilla
ice cream & raspberries)

L'automne
Autumn

Salade de chèvre chaud
(Grilled goat's cheese salad)
Sauvignon Blanc

Confit de cuisse de canard
(Crisp fried duck leg)
avec
Purée de carottes et cumin
(Carrot and cumin puree)
&
Endives braisées
(Braised witlof)
St Emillion or Pinot Gris

Vacherin aux fruits de la passion
(Meringues with passionfruit)
Gewürztraminer

L'hiver
Winter

Pâté de campagne
(Country-style terrine)
Pinot Blanc or Beaujolais

Lapin aux pruneaux
(Rabbit casserole with prunes)
avec
Choux de bruxelles à l'auvergnate
(Pan-fried brussels sprouts
with chestnuts & bacon)
Pommerol

Fondant au chocolat
(Soft-centred chocolate pudding)
Banyuls

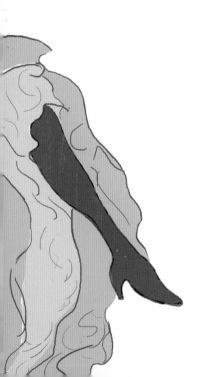

A Lyonnaise bouchon

Parfait de foies de volaille
(Chicken liver parfait
with Armagnac butter)
Beaujolais

Pot-au-feu
&
Haricots verts aux échalotes
(Green beans with shallots)
Beaujolais

Mousse au chocolat noir
(Dark chocolate mousse)
Muscat

A Parisienne soirée

Huîtres mignonette
(Oysters with black pepper
& shallot vinegar)
Chablis

Bisque de homard
(Lobster bisque)
Dry sherry

Côte de porc charcutiere
(Grilled pork chop with
mustard & cornichon sauce)
&
Chou-fleur a la polonaise
(Cauliflower with
crisp breadcrumbs & egg)
Chardonnay

Brie de Meaux fromage
Chardonnay

Crème brûlée
(Caramelised custard)
Sautérnes

A long lunch in Provence

Soupe de poissons
(Fish soup)

Brandade de morue
(Salt cod & potato puree)

Poulet aux quarante gousses d'ail
(Pot-roasted chicken with
40 cloves of garlic)

Ratatouille
(Stewed Provençal vegetables)

A Provençal rosé matches
the three dishes perfectly

Tarte aux pignons et agrumes
(Pinenut & confit citrus tart)
Late harvest botrytized Semillon

233

A little about me

I started my career in the pot wash of a hotel 20 years ago. At that time every young, eager chef cut his or her teeth in the 'plunge'. I worked my way through the ranks, learning the French fundamentals. The head chef was old school—we did everything on site, including baking and butchery in the proper way, the French way.

Ok, I'm not French, but I am very much a Francophile in the food sense. I admire a nation that is so passionate about its individual regions and what they produce. The French boom with pride as they argue about the specialities produced in their own region, but always respect each other's.

I vividly remember my days of training in Dunedin, learning seemingly obscure terminology, sauces and garnishes. Ironically, it's this that fuels my passion for French food. Sometimes I feel my job is part historian, part chef. In saying this, I recognise that some of the traditional food has little merit and should be regarded just as historical reference. I am interested in the classics that have fallen out of favour due to our changing tastes, values and lifestyles. Why don't we eat veal head anymore, for instance? Is it too graphic? Don't we want to be confronted with the reality of death in our lives?

It's this type of dish that is a bistro staple, an example of kitchen economy. The whole beast is brought in, the head is used for a *tête de veau gribiche*, the feet and bones for stock, the offal used for dishes such as *foie de veau au poivre* or *ris de veau* and the prime cuts roasted or grilled. It's this economy which created the great dishes of France.

My love of home cooking was born out of necessity. Coming from a family of eight, cooking was more like an organised production line. I was raised in the country on a small farm that was run just for our family's needs, not for financial gain—like many small French farms. I guess we were a cow short of self-sufficiency. We had a vegetable patch as large as most house sites, a stone fruit and apple orchard, pigs, chickens, ducks and sheep. There was always seasonal produce to pick straight from the garden, a larder full of preserves, conserves, fresh baked goods and a fridge brimming with home-grown meat.

This all sounds great, but with it came great responsibility. We all had tasks that needed to be done each day. Tending to the welfare of the livestock was paramount—bailing hay for the sheep, crushing grain for the pigs, securing the poultry from predators and tending to orphan lambs. Weeding the garden was reserved as a punishment.

Those were great days, a grounding in nature and the origins of food. I've left the rural life behind, but that doesn't stop me getting excited about the changing seasons and the produce they bring. I replicate this enthusiasm in the big city at La Brasserie, cooking honest, uncomplicated fare in true bistro style and giving upmost respect to the ingredients.

I have worked in my fair share of fine dining establishments where the goal is to manipulate the produce into culinary feats of art. These are technical skills in which every chef is trained and can be learned. It is having the confidence to rely on simplicity that has taken the longest to master.

Glossary

BOUQUET GARNI: A small bundle of herbs tied in leek or muslin so they can be easily extracted from simmered dishes. It consists of:
1 bay leaf
3 sprigs of thyme
4 parsley stalks
6 peppercorns

FLAMBÉ: To set alight, with the intention of removing alcohol content.

LARDONS: Thick-cut streaky bacon that has been cut into small pieces, usually batons.

OIGNON CLOUTE: A small peeled onion studded with four or five cloves and a bay leaf.

QUATRE ÉPICES: A fragrant spice blend commonly used in charcutiere preparations. It consists of:
50g (1¾oz) ground white pepper
50g (1¾oz) ground cinnamon
25g (¾oz) ground nutmeg
20g (⅔oz) ground cloves

SALT: Fleur de sel is a hand-harvested salt obtained by scraping off only the top layer from salt pans. It is a delicate crystal that dissolves quicker and has a less salty taste than regular salt. Used for finishing dishes.

SALTPETRE: Saltpetre (potassium nitrate) is used to dry-cure and preserve foods, particularly meats.

Index of Recipes

Index of recipes 239

Eugène Atget

Between 1898 and 1927 the photographer Eugène Atget (1857–1927) spend his days documenting the streets, laneways, parks and buildings of Paris, creating a remarkable archive of photographs documenting the city. He used a large-format view camera and left over 8,000 glass negatives. Atget photographs reproduced here are on: **page 6** Café 'A l'Homme Armé', 25 rue des Blancs-Manteaux, 1900; **page 17** 'Au Coq Hardi', 18 quai de la Mégisserie, 1902; **page 30** 'Maison Mailliard', Les Halles, 1911; **page 59** Porteuse de pains, 1899; **page 70** Street of posters; **page 92** Boutique, 25 rue Charlemagne, 1911; **page 108** Cour du Dragon, 50 rue de Rennes, 1900; **page 153** Voiture de brasseur, 1910; **page 160** Boutique de fruits et légumes, rue Mouffetard, 1925; **page 186** 'Au Tambour', 63 quai de la Tournelle, 1908; **page 216** Boulangerie, 48 rue Descartes, 1911.

Our thanks to Accoutrement, Jakk Armstrong, Sharon Mann of Blanc-Léger and Honey Bee Homewares.

First published in 2011 by New Holland Publishers (Australia) Pty Ltd
Sydney • Auckland • London • Cape Town
www.newholland.com.au

1/66 Gibbes Street Chatswood NSW 2067 Australia • 218 Lake Road Northcote Auckland New Zealand • 86 Edgware Road London W2 2EA United Kingdom • 80 McKenzie Street Cape Town 8001 South Africa

A record of this book is available at the National Library of Australia

ISBN 9781742571331

Publisher: Diane Jardine
Publishing manager: Lliane Clarke
Senior editor: Mary Trewby
Design concept: Emma Gough
Designers: Emma Gough, Celeste Vlok and Erin Farrugia
Cover design: Celeste Vlok
Front cover photograph: Celeste Vlok
Photographer: Graeme Gillies
Stylist: Mandy Biffin
Production manager: Olga Dementiev
Printer: Toppan Leefung Printing (China) Ltd

10 9 8 7 6 5 4 3 2 1